Stories of Success:

Phil the Fiddler
(Illustrated)

Stories of Success:

Phil the Fiddler
(Illustrated)

Horatio Alger, Jr.

Sumner Books
Hermosa Beach, CA

TABLE OF CONTENTS

A NOTE FROM THE PUBLISHER

Once crowned "America's most influential writer," Horatio Alger is hardly known today. Those who are familiar with him think "rags to riches," and that's about it. Most young people have never heard of him.

What an opportunity!

More than a hundred years before our contemporary self-help movement, Horatio Alger paved the way with his vivid illustrations of the keys to success and happiness. Today, Sumner Books is excited to introduce a new generation of Americans to some of the most inspirational stories ever written. Regardless of your age, you simply cannot read a Horatio Alger book without coming away with a good feeling.

Alger's books initially sold in the millions and then the tens of millions and finally the hundreds of millions. In fact, the Chicago Daily News once called Horatio Alger "America's best-selling author of all time." Sumner Books is committed to bringing to life this best-selling collection in the form of audiobooks read by professional actors and recorded with audio engineers in our studio. Our revised e-books, each with a detailed table of contents and colored illustrations, are professionally edited, including the occasional updating of phrases to make the books as easy to read today as they were when they were first published between 1865 and 1900.

Long after his death in 1899, the magazine Publishers Weekly wrote: "To call Horatio Alger Jr. America's most influential writer may seem like an overstatement ... but ... only Benjamin Franklin meant as much to the formation of the American popular mind."

Our goal is to bring back some of the influence that Alger exerted on millions of young people in America. Yes, it's retro; it's counterintuitive and totally contrary to the cynicism that has become a part of American culture. But we are proud to be leading a movement that is as positive and uplifting as the last pages of a Horatio Alger story.

Rick Newcombe
President
Sumner Books

Stories of Success

CHAPTER I

PHIL THE FIDDLER

"Viva Garibaldi!" sang a young Italian boy in an uptown street, accompanying himself on a violin which, from its battered appearance, seemed to have met with hard usage.

As the young singer is to be the hero of my story, I will pause to describe him. He was twelve years old, but small of his age. His complexion was a brilliant olive, with the dark eyes peculiar to his race, and his hair black. In spite of the dirt, his face was strikingly handsome, especially when lighted up by a smile, as was often the case, for in spite of the hardships of his lot, and these were neither few nor light, Filippo was naturally merry and light-hearted.

He wore a velveteen jacket, and pantaloons which atoned, by their extra length, for the holes resulting from hard usage and antiquity. His shoes, which appeared to be wholly unacquainted with blacking, were, like his pantaloons, two or three sizes too large for him, making it necessary for him to shuffle along ungracefully.

It was now ten o'clock in the morning. Two hours had elapsed since Filippo, or Phil, as I shall call him, for the benefit of my readers unfamiliar with Italian names, had left the miserable home in Crosby Street, where he and forty other boys lived in charge of a middle-aged Italian, known as the padrone. Of this person, and the relations between him and the boys, I shall hereafter speak. At present I propose to accompany Phil.

Though he had wandered about, singing and playing, for two hours, Phil had not yet received a penny. This made him somewhat uneasy, for he knew that at night he must carry home a satisfactory sum to the padrone, or he would be brutally beaten; and poor Phil knew from sad experience that this hard taskmaster had no mercy in such cases.

The block in which he stood was adjacent to Fifth Avenue, and was lined on either side with brown-stone houses. It was quiet, and but few passed through it during the busy hours of the day. But Phil's hope was that some money might be thrown him from a window of some of the fine houses before which he played, but he seemed likely to be disappointed, for he played ten minutes without apparently attracting any attention. He was about to change his

---

position, when the basement door of one of the houses opened, and a servant came out, bareheaded, and approached him. Phil regarded her with distrust, for he was often ordered away as a nuisance. He stopped playing, and, hugging his violin closely, regarded her watchfully.

"You're to come in," said the girl abruptly.

"Che cosa volete?"(1) said Phil, suspiciously.

 (1) "What do you want?"

"I don't understand your Italian rubbish," said the girl. "You're to come into the house."

In general, boys of Phil's class are slow in learning English. After months, and even years sometimes, their knowledge is limited to a few words or phrases. On the other hand, they pick up French readily, and as many of them, en route for America, spend some weeks, or months, in the French metropolis, it is common to find them able to speak the language somewhat. Phil, however, was an exception, and could manage to speak English a little, though not as well as he could understand it.

"What for I go?" he asked, a little distrustfully.

"My young master wants to hear you play on your fiddle," said the servant. "He's sick, and can't come out."

"All right!" said Phil, using one of the first English phrases he had caught. "I will go."

"Come along, then."

Phil followed his guide into the basement, thence up two flight of stairs, and along a handsome hall into a chamber. The little fiddler, who had never before been invited into a fine house, looked with admiration at the handsome furniture, and especially at the pictures upon the wall, for, like most of his nation, he had a love for whatever was beautiful, whether in nature or art.

The chamber had two occupants. One, a boy of twelve years, was lying in a bed, propped up by pillows. His thin, pale face spoke of long sickness, and contrasted vividly with the brilliant brown face of the little Italian boy, who seemed the perfect picture of health. Sitting beside the bed was a lady of middle age and pleasant expression. It was easy to see by the resemblance that she was the mother of the sick boy.

Phil looked from one to the other, uncertain what was required of him.

"Can you speak English?" asked Mrs. Leigh.

—

4

"Si, signora, a little," answered our hero.

"My son is sick, and would like to hear you play a little."

"And sing, too," added the sick boy, from the bed.

Phil struck up the song he had been singing in the street, a song well known to all who have stopped to listen to the boys of his class, with the refrain, "Viva Garibaldi." His voice was clear and melodious, and in spite of the poor quality of his instrument, he sang with so much feeling that the effect was agreeable.

The sick boy listened with evident pleasure, for he, too, had a taste for music.

"I wish I could understand Italian," he said, "I think it must be a good song."

"Perhaps he can sing some English song," suggested Mrs. Leigh.

"Can you sing in English?" she asked.

Phil hesitated a moment, and then broke into the common street ditty, "Shoe fly, don't bouder me," giving a quaint sound to the words by his Italian accent.

"Do you know any more?" asked Henry Leigh, when our hero had finished.

"Not English," said Phil, shaking his head.

"You ought to learn more."

"I can play more," said Phil, "but I know not the words."

"Then play some tunes."

Thereupon the little Italian struck up "Yankee Doodle," which he played with spirit and evident enjoyment.

"Do you know the name of that?" asked Henry.

Phil shook his head.

"It is 'Yankee Doodle.'"

Phil tried to pronounce it, but the words in his mouth had a droll sound, and made them laugh.

"How old are you?" asked Henry.

"Twelve years."

"Then you are quite as old as I am."

"I wish you were as well and strong as he seems to be," said Mrs. Leigh, sighing, as she looked at Henry's pale face.

That was little likely to be. Always a delicate child, Henry had a year previous contracted a cold, which had attacked his lungs, and had gradually increased until there seemed little doubt that in the long struggle with disease nature must succumb, and early death ensue.

"How long have you been in this country?"

"Un anno."

"How long is that?"

"A year," said Henry. "I know that, because 'annus' means a year in Latin."

"Si, signor, a year," said Phil.

"And where do you come from?"

"Da Napoli."

"That means from Naples, I suppose."

"Si, signor."

Most of the little Italian musicians to be found in our streets are brought from Calabria, the southern portion of Italy, where they are purchased from their parents, for a fixed sum, or rate of annual payment. But it is usual for them when questioned, to say that they come from Naples, that being the principal city in that portion of Italy, or indeed in the entire kingdom.

"Who do you live with," continued Henry.

"With the padrone."

"And who is the padrone?"

"He take care of me—he bring me from Italy."

"Is he kind to you?"

Phil shrugged his shoulders.

"He beat me sometimes," he answered.

"Beats you? What for?"

"If I bring little money."

"Does he beat you hard?"

"Si, signor, with a stick."

"He must be a bad man," said Henry, indignantly.

"How much money must you carry home?"

"Two dollars."

"But it isn't your fault, if people will not give you money."

"Non importa. He beat me."

"He ought to be beaten himself."

Phil shrugged his shoulders. Like most boys of his class, to him the padrone seemed all-powerful. The idea that his oppressive taskmaster should be punished for his cruelty had never dawned upon him. Knowing nothing of any law that would protect him, he submitted to it as a necessity, from which there was no escape except

—

6

by running away. He had not come to that yet, but some of his companions had done so, and he might some day.

After this conversation he played another tune. Mrs. Leigh drew out her purse, and gave him fifty cents. Phil took his fiddle under his arm, and, following the servant, who now reappeared, emerged into the street, and moved onward.

CHAPTER II

PHIL AND HIS PROTECTOR

To a certain extent Phil was his own master; that is, he was at liberty to wander where he liked, provided he did not neglect his business, and returned to the lodging-house at night with the required sum of money. But woe to him if he were caught holding back any of the money for his own use. In that case, he would be beaten, and sent to bed without his supper, while the padrone, according to the terms of his contract with the distant parent would withhold from the amount due the latter ten times the sum kept by the boy. In the middle of the day he was allowed to spend three cents for bread, which was the only dinner allowed him. Of course, the boys were tempted to regale themselves more luxuriously, but they incurred a great risk in doing so. Sometimes the padrone followed them secretly, or employed others to do so, and so was able to detect them. Besides, they traveled, in general, by twos and threes, and the system of espionage was encouraged by the padrone. So mutual distrust was inspired, and the fear of being reported made the boys honest.

Phil left the house of Mr. Leigh in good spirits. Though he had earned nothing before, the fifty cents he had just received made a good beginning, and inspired in him the hope of getting together enough to save him a beating, for one night at least.

He walked down toward Sixth Avenue, and turning the corner walked down town. At length he paused in front of a tobacconist's shop, and began to play. But he had chosen an unfortunate time and place. The tobacconist had just discovered a deficiency in his money account, which he suspected to be occasioned by the dishonesty of his assistant. In addition to this he had risen with a headache, so that he was in a decidedly bad humor. Music had no charms for him at that moment, and he no sooner heard the first strains of Phil's violin than he rushed from the shop bareheaded, and dashed impetuously at the young fiddler.

"Get away from my shop, you little vagabond!" he cried. "If I had my way, you should all be sent out of the country."

Phil was quick to take a hint. He saw the menace in the shopkeeper's eyes, and, stopping abruptly, ran farther down the

---

8

street, hugging his fiddle, which he was afraid the angry tobacconist might seize and break. This, to him, would be an irreparable misfortune and subject him to a severe punishment, though the fault would not be his.

Next he strolled into a side street, and began to play in front of some dwelling-houses. Two or three young children, who had been playing in the street, gathered about him, and one of them gave him a penny. They were clamorous for another tune, but Phil could not afford to work for nothing, and, seeing no prospects of additional pay, took his violin, and walked away, much to the regret of his young auditors, who, though not rich, were appreciative. They followed him to the end of the block, hoping that he would play again, but they were disappointed.

Phil played two or three times more, managing to obtain in all twenty-five cents additional. He reached the corner of Thirteenth Street just as the large public school, known as the Thirteenth Street School, was dismissed for its noon intermission.

"Give us a tune, Johnny," cried Edward Eustis, one of the oldest boys.

"Yes, a tune," joined in several others.

This was an invitation to which Phil was always willing to respond. Besides, he knew from experience that boys were more generous, in proportion to their means, than those of larger growth, and he hoped to get enough from the crowd around him to increase his store to a dollar.

The boys gathered around the little minstrel, who struck up an Italian tune, but without the words.

"Sing, sing!" cried the boys.

Phil began to sing. His clear, fresh voice produced a favorable impression upon the boys.

"He's a bully singer," said one. "I can't sing much better myself."

"You sing! Your singing would be enough to scare a dozen tom cats."

"Then we should be well matched. Look here, Johnny, can't you sing something in English?"

Phil, in response to this request, played and sang "Shoo Fly!" which suiting the boys' taste, he was called upon to repeat.

The song being finished, Edward Eustis took off his cap, and went around the circle.

—

9

"Now, boys, you have a chance to show your liberality," he said. "I'll start the collection with five cents."

"That's ahead of me," said James Marcus. "Justice to a large and expensive family will prevent me contributing anything more than two cents."

"The smallest favors thankfully received," said Edward.

"Then take that, and be thankful," said Tom Lane, dropping in a penny.

"I haven't got any money," said Frank Gaylord, "but here's an apple;" and he dropped a large red apple into the cap.

Phil; watching with interest the various contributions, was best pleased with the last. The money he must carry to the padrone. The apple he might keep for himself, and it would vary agreeably his usual meager fare.

"The biggest contribution yet," said Edward.

"Here, Sprague, you are liberal. What'll you give?"

"My note at ninety days."

"You might fail before it comes due."

"Then take three cents. 'Tis all I have; 'I can no more, though poor the offering be.'"

"Oh, don't quote Shakespeare."

"It isn't Shakespeare; it's Milton."

"Just as much one as the other."

"Here, Johnny," said Edward, after going the rounds, "hold your hands, and I'll pour out the money. You can retire from business now on a fortune."

Phil was accustomed to be addressed as Johnny, that being the generic name for boy in New York. He deposited the money in his pocket, and, taking his fiddle, played once more in acknowledgment of the donation. The boys now dispersed, leaving Phil to go on his way. He took out the apple with the intention of eating it, when a rude boy snatched it from his hand.

"Give it back," said Phil, angrily.

"Don't you wish you may get it?" said the other, holding it out of his reach.

The young musician had little chance of redress, his antagonist was a head taller than himself, and, besides, he would not have dared lay down his fiddle to fight, lest it might be broken.

"Give it to me," he said, stamping his foot.

"I mean to eat it myself," said the other, coolly. "It's too good for the likes of you."

"You're a thief."

"Don't you call me names, you little Italian ragamuffin, or I'll hit you," said the other, menacingly.

"It is my apple."

"I'm going to eat it."

But the speaker was mistaken. As he held the apple above his head, it was suddenly snatched from him. He looked around angrily, and confronted Edward Eustis, who, seeing Phil's trouble from a little distance, had at once come to his rescue.

"What did you do that for?" demanded the thief.

"What did you take the boy's apple for?"

"Because I felt like it."

"Then I took it from you for the same reason."

"Do you want to fight?" blustered the rowdy.

"Not particularly."

"Then hand me back that apple," returned the other.

"Thank you; I shall only hand it to the rightful owner—that little Italian boy. Are you not ashamed to rob him?"

"Do you want to get hit?"

"I wouldn't advise you to do it."

The rowdy looked at the boy who confronted him. Edward was slightly smaller, but there was a determined look in his eye which the bully, who, like those of his class generally, was a coward at heart, did not like. He mentally decided that it would be safer not to provoke him.

"Come here, Johnny, and take your apple," said Edward.

Phil advanced, and received back his property with satisfaction.

"You'd better eat it now. I'll see that he doesn't disturb you."

Phil followed the advice of his new friend promptly. He had eaten nothing since seven o'clock, and then only a piece of dry bread and cheese, and the apple, a rare luxury, he did not fail to relish. His would-be robber scowled at him meanwhile, for he had promised himself the pleasure of dispatching the fruit. Edward stood by till the apple was eaten, and then turned away. The rowdy made a movement as if to follow Phil, but Edward quickly detected him, and came back.

"Don't you dare touch him," he said, significantly, "or you'll have to settle accounts with me. Do you see that policeman? I am

---

going to ask him to have an eye on you. You'd better look out for yourself."

The other turned at the caution, and seeing the approach of one of the Metropolitan police quickly vanished. He had a wholesome fear of these guardians of the public peace, and did not care to court their attention.

Edward turned away, but in a moment felt a hand tugging at his coat. Looking around, he saw that it was Phil.

"Grazia, signore," said Phil, gratefully.

"I suppose that means 'Thank you'?"

Phil nodded.

"All right, Johnny! I am glad I was by to save you from that bully."

CHAPTER III

GIACOMO

After eating the apple Phil decided to buy his frugal dinner. He, therefore, went into a baker's shop, and bought two penny rolls and a piece of cheese. It was not a very luxurious repast, but with the apple it was better than usual. A few steps from the shop door he met another Italian boy, who was bound to the same padrone.

"How much money have you, Giacomo?" asked Phil, speaking, of course, in his native tongue.

"Forty cents. How much have you?"

"A dollar and twenty cents."

"You are very lucky, Filippo."

"A rich signora gave me fifty cents for playing to her sick boy. Then I sang for some schoolboys, and they gave me some money."

"I am afraid the padrone will beat me to-night."

"He has not beat me for a week."

"Have you had dinner, Filippo?"

"Yes, I had some bread and cheese, and an apple."

"Did you buy the apple?"

"No; one of the schoolboys gave it to me. It was very good," said Phil, in a tone of enjoyment. "I had not eaten one for a long time."

"Nor I. Do you remember, Filippo, the oranges we had in Italy?"

"I remember them well."

"I was happy then," said Giacomo, sighing. "There was no padrone to beat me, and I could run about and play. Now I have to sing and play all day. I am so tired sometimes,—so tired, Filippo."

"You are not so strong as I, Giacomo," said Phil, looking with some complacency at his own stout limbs.

"Don't you get tired, Filippo?"

"Yes, often; but I don't care so much for that. But I don't like the winter."

"I thought I should die with cold sometimes last winter," said Giacomo, shuddering. "Do you ever expect to go back to Italy, Filippo?"

"Sometime."

"I wish I could go now. I should like to see my dear mother and my sisters."

"And your father?"

"I don't want to see him," said Giacomo, bitterly. "He sold me to the padrone. My mother wept bitterly when I went away, but my father only thought of the money."

Filippo and Giacomo were from the same town in Calabria. They were the sons of Italian peasants who had been unable to resist the offers of the padrone, and for less than a hundred dollars each had sold his son into the cruelest slavery. The boys were torn from their native hills, from their families, and in a foreign land were doomed to walk the streets from fourteen to sixteen hours in every twenty-four, gathering money from which they received small benefit. Many times, as they trudged through the streets, weary and hungry, sometimes cold, they thought with homesick sadness of the sunny fields in which their earliest years had been passed, but the hard realities of the life they were now leading soon demanded their attention.

Naturally light-hearted, Filippo, or Phil, bore his hard lot more cheerfully than some of his comrades. But Giacomo was more delicate, and less able to bear want and fatigue. His livelier comrade cheered him up, and Giacomo always felt better after talking with Phil.

As the two boys were walking together, a heavy hand was laid on the shoulder of each, and a harsh voice said: "Is this the way you waste your time, little rascals?"

Both boys started, and looking up, recognized the padrone. He was a short man, very dark with fierce black eyes and a sinister countenance. It was his habit to walk about the streets from time to time, and keep a watch, unobserved, upon his young apprentices, if they may be so called. If he found them loitering about, or neglecting their work, they were liable to receive a sharp reminder.

The boys were both startled at his sudden appearance, but after the first start, Phil, who was naturally courageous, recovered his self-possession. Not so with Giacomo, who was the more afraid because he knew he had gained but little money thus far.

"We are not wasting our time, padrone," said Phil, looking up fearlessly.

"We will see about that. How long have you been together?"

"Only five minutes."

"How much money have you, Filippo?"

"A dollar and twenty cents."

"Good; you have done well. And how is it with you, Giacomo?"

"I have forty cents."

"Then you have been idle," said the padrone, frowning.

"No, signore," said the boy, trembling. "I have played, but they did not give me much money."

"It is not his fault," said Phil, coming boldly to the defense of his friend.

"Attend to your own affairs, little scrape-grace," said the padrone, roughly. "He might have got as much as you."

"No, padrone; I was lucky. A kind lady gave me fifty cents."

"That is not my affair. I don't care where you get the money. But if you don't bring home all I expect, you shall feel the stick."

These last words were addressed to Giacomo, who understood their import only too well. In the miserable lodging where he herded with thirty or forty others scarcely a night passed without the brutal punishment of one or more unfortunate boys, who had been unsuccessful in bringing home enough to satisfy the rapacity of the padrone. But of this an account will hereafter be given.

"Now, go to work, both of you," said the padrone, harshly.

The two boys separated. Giacomo went uptown, while Phil kept on his way toward the Astor House. The padrone made his way to the nearest liquor shop, where he invested a portion of the money wrung from the hard earnings of his young apprentices.

Toward the close of the afternoon Phil found himself in front of the Astor House. He had played several times, but was not fortunate in finding liberal auditors. He had secured but ten cents during this time, and it seemed doubtful whether he would reach the sum he wanted. He crossed over to the City Hall Park, and, feeling tired, sat down on one of the benches. Two bootblacks were already seated upon it.

"Play us a tune, Johnny," said one.

"Will you give me pennies?" asked Phil doubtfully, for he did not care, with such a severe taskmaster, to work for nothing.

"Yes, we'll give you pennies."

Upon this, Phil struck up a tune.

"Where's your monkey?" asked one of the boys.

"I have no monkey."

"If you want a monkey, here's one for you," said Tim Rafferty, putting his hand on his companion's shoulder.

"He's too big," said Phil, laughing.

"Hould yer gab, Tim Rafferty," said the other. "It's you that'll make a better monkey nor I. Say, Johnny, do you pay your monkeys well?"

"Give me my pennies," said Phil, with an eye to business.

"Play another tune, then."

Phil obeyed directions. When he had finished, a contribution was taken up, but it only amounted to seven cents. However, considering the character of the audience, this was as much as could be expected.

"How much have you made to-day, Johnny?" asked Tim.

"A dollar," said Phil.

"A dollar! That's more nor I have made. I tell you what, boys, I think I'll buy a fiddle myself. I'll make more money that way than blackin' boots."

"A great fiddler you'd make, Tim Rafferty."

"Can't I play, then? Lend me your fiddle, Johnny, till I try it a little."

Phil shook his head.

"Give it to me now; I won't be hurtin' it."

"You'll break it."

"Then I'll pay for it."

"It isn't mine."

"Whose is it, then?"

"The padrone's."

"And who's the padrone?"

"The man I live with. If the fiddle is broken, he will beat me."

"Then he's an ould haythen, and you may tell him so, with Tim Rafferty's compliments. But I won't hurt it."

Phil, however, feared to trust the violin in unskillful hands. He knew the penalty if any harm befell it, and he had no mind to run the risk. So he rose from the seat, and withdrew to a little distance, Tim Rafferty following, for, though he cared little at first, he now felt determined to try the fiddle.

"If you don't give it to me I'll put a head on you," he said.

"You shall not have it," said Phil, firmly, for he, too, could be determined.

"The little chap's showing fight," said Tim's companion. "Look out, Tim; he'll mash you."

"I can fight him wid one hand," said Tim.

He advanced upon our young hero, who, being much smaller, would probably have been compelled to yield to superior force but for an interference entirely unexpected by Tim.

CHAPTER IV

AN INVITATION TO SUPPER

Tim had raised his fist to strike the young fiddler, when he was suddenly pushed aside with considerable force, and came near measuring his length on the ground.

"Who did that?" he cried, angrily, recovering his equilibrium.

"I did it," said a calm voice.

Tim recognized in the speaker Paul Hoffman, whom some of my readers will remember as "Paul the Peddler." Paul was proprietor of a necktie stand below the Astor House, and was just returning home to supper.

He was a brave and manly boy, and his sympathies were always in favor of the oppressed. He had met Phil before, and talked with him, and seeing him in danger came to his assistance.

"What made you push me?" demanded Tim, fiercely.

"What were you going to do to him?" rejoined Paul, indicating the Italian boy.

"I was only goin' to borrer his fiddle."

"He would have broken it," said Phil.

"You don't know how to play," said Paul. "You would have broken his fiddle, and then he would be beaten."

"I would pay for it if I did," said Tim.

"You say so, but you wouldn't. Even if you did, it would take time, and the boy would have suffered."

"What business is that of yours?" demanded Tim, angrily.

"It is always my business when I see a big boy teasing a little one."

"You'll get hurt some day," said Tim, suddenly.

"Not by you," returned Paul, not particularly alarmed.

Tim would have gladly have punished Paul on the spot for his interference, but he did not consider it prudent to provoke hostilities. Paul was as tall as himself, and considerably stronger. He therefore wisely confined himself to threatening words.

"Come along with me, Phil," said Paul, kindly, to the little fiddler.

"Thank you for saving me," said Phil, gratefully. "The padrone would beat me if the fiddle was broke."

18

"Never mind about thanks, Phil. Tim is a bully with small boys, but he is a coward among large ones. Have you had any supper?"

"No," said Phil.

"Won't you come home and take supper with me?"

Phil hesitated.

"You are kind," he said, "but I fear the padrone."

"What will he do to you?"

"He will beat me if I don't bring home enough money."

"How much more must you get?"

"Sixty cents."

"You can play better after a good supper. Come along; I won't keep you long."

Phil made no more objection. He was a healthy boy, and his wanderings had given him a good appetite. So he thanked Paul, and walked along by his side. One object Paul had in inviting him was, the fear that Tim Rafferty might take advantage of his absence to renew his assault upon Phil, and with better success than before.

"How old are you, Phil?" he asked.

"Twelve years."

"And who taught you to play?"

"No one. I heard the other boys play, and so I learned."

"Do you like it?"

"Sometimes; but I get tired of it."

"I don't wonder. I should think playing day after day might tire you. What are you going to do when you become a man?"

Phil shrugged his shoulders.

"I don't know," he said. "I think I'll go back to Italy."

"Have you any relations there?"

"I have a mother and two sisters."

"And a father?"

"Yes, a father."

"Why did they let you come away?"

"The padrone gave my father money."

"Don't you hear anything from home?"

"No, signore."

"I am not a signore," said Paul, smiling. "You may call me Paul. Is that an Italian name?"

"Me call it Paolo."

"That sounds queer to me. What's James in Italian?"

"Giacomo."

19

"Then I have a little brother Giacomo."

"How old is he?"

"Eight years old."

"My sister Bettina is eight years. I wish I could see her."

"You will see her again some day, Phil. You will get rich in America, and go back to sunny Italy."

"The padrone takes all my money."

"You'll get away from the old rascal some day. Keep up good courage, Phil, and all will come right. But here we are. Follow me upstairs, and I will introduce you to my mother and Giacomo," said Paul, laughing at the Italian name he had given his little brother.

Mrs. Hoffman and Jimmy looked with some surprise at the little fiddler as he entered with Paul.

"Mother," said Paul, "this is one of my friends, whom I have invited to take supper with us."

"He is welcome," said Mrs. Hoffman, kindly. "Have you ever spoken to us of him?"

"I am not sure. His name is Phil—Phil the fiddler, we call him."

"Filippo," said the young musician.

"We will call you Phil; it is easier to speak," said Paul. "This is my little brother Jimmy. He is a great artist."

"Now you are laughing at me, Paul," said the little boy.

"Well, he is going to be a great artist some day, if he isn't one yet. Do you think, Jimmy, you could draw Phil, here, with his fiddle?"

"I think I could," said the little boy, slowly, looking carefully at their young guest; "but it would take some time."

"Perhaps Phil will come some day, and give you a sitting."

"Will you come?" asked Jimmy.

"I will come some day."

Meanwhile Mrs. Hoffman was preparing supper. Since Paul had become proprietor of the necktie stand, as described in the last volume, they were able to live with less regard to economy than before. So, when the table was spread, it presented quite a tempting appearance. Beefsteak, rolls, fried potatoes, coffee, and preserves graced the board.

"Supper is ready, Paul," said his mother, when all was finished.

"Here, Phil, you may sit here at my right hand," said Paul. "I will put your violin where it will not be injured."

Phil sat down as directed, not without feeling a little awkward, yet with a sense of anticipated pleasure. Accustomed to bread and cheese alone, the modest repast before him seemed like a royal feast. The meat especially attracted him, for he had not tasted any for months, indeed seldom in his life, for in Italy it is seldom eaten by the class to which Phil's parents belonged.

"Let me give you some meat, Phil," said Paul. "Now, shall we drink the health of the padrone in coffee?"

"I will not drink his health," said Phil. "He is a bad man."

"Who is the padrone?" asked Jimmy, curiously.

"He is my master. He sends me out to play for money."

"And must you give all the money you make to him?"

"Yes; if I do not bring much money, he will beat me."

"Then he must be a bad man. Why do you live with him?"

"He bought me from my father."

"He bought you?" repeated Jimmy, puzzled.

"He hires him for so much money," explained Paul.

"But why did your father let you go with a bad man?" asked Jimmy.

"He wanted the money," said Phil. "He cared more for money than for me."

What wonder that the boys sold into such cruel slavery should be estranged from the fathers who for a few paltry ducats sell the liberty and happiness of their children. Even where the contract is for a limited terms of years, the boys in five cases out of ten are not returned at the appointed time. A part, unable to bear the hardships and privations of the life upon which they enter, are swept off by death, while of those that survive, a part are weaned from their homes, or are not permitted to go back.

"You must not ask too many questions, Jimmy." said Mrs. Hoffman, fearing that he might awaken sad thoughts in the little musician.

She was glad to see that Phil ate with a good appetite. In truth he relished the supper, which was the best he remembered to have tasted for many a long day.

"Is Italy like America?" asked Jimmy, whose curiosity was excited to learn something of Phil's birthplace.

"It is much nicer," said Phil, with a natural love of country. "There are olive trees and orange trees, and grapes—very many."

"Are there really orange trees? Have you seen them grow?"

"I have picked them from the trees many times."

"I should like that, but I don't care for olives."

"They are good, too."

"I should like the grapes."

"There are other things in Italy which you would like better, Jimmy," said Paul.

"What do you mean, Paul?"

"The galleries of fine paintings."

"Yes, I should like to see them. Have you seen them?"

Phil shook his head. The picture galleries are in the cities, and not in the country district where he was born.

"Sometime, when I am rich, we will all go to Italy, Jimmy; then, if Phil is at home, we will go and see him."

"I should like that, Paul."

Though Jimmy was not yet eight years old, he had already exhibited a remarkable taste for drawing, and without having received any instruction, could copy any ordinary picture with great exactness. It was the little boy's ambition to become an artist, and in this ambition he was encouraged by Paul, who intended, as soon as he could afford it, to engage an instructor for Jimmy.

CHAPTER V

ON THE FERRY BOAT

When supper was over, Phil bethought himself that his day's work was not yet over. He had still a considerable sum to obtain before he dared go home, if such a name can be given to the miserable tenement in Crosby Street where he herded with his companions. But before going he wished to show his gratitude to Paul for his protection and the supper which he had so much and so unexpectedly enjoyed.

"Shall I play for you?" he asked, taking his violin from the top of the bureau, where Paul had placed it.

"Will you?" asked Jimmy, his eyes lighting up with pleasure.

"We should be very glad to hear you," said Mrs. Hoffman.

Phil played his best, for he felt that he was playing for friends. After a short prelude, he struck into an Italian song. Though the words were unintelligible, the little party enjoyed the song.

"Bravo, Phil!" said Paul. "You sing almost as well as I do."

Jimmy laughed.

"You sing about as well as you draw," said the little boy.

"There you go again with your envy and jealousy," said Paul, in an injured tone. "Others appreciate me better."

"Sing something, and we will judge of your merits," said his mother.

"Not now," said Paul, shaking his head. "My feelings are too deeply injured. But if he has time, Phil will favor us with another song."

So the little fiddler once more touched the strings of his violin, and sang the hymn of Garibaldi.

**The street musicians play the "Hymn of Garibaldi,"
which was written in honor of Italian General Garibaldi.**

"He has a beautiful voice," said Mrs. Hoffman to Paul.

"Yes, Phil sings much better than most of his class. Shall I bring him up here again?"

"Any time, Paul. We shall always be glad to see him."

Here Phil took his cap and prepared to depart.

"Good-by," he said in English. "I thank you all for your kindness."

"Will you come again?" said Mrs. Hoffman. "We shall be glad to have you."

"Do come," pleaded Jimmy, who had taken a fancy to the dark-eyed Italian boy, whose brilliant brown complexion contrasted strongly with his own pale face and blue eyes.

These words gave Phil a strange pleasure. Since his arrival in America he had become accustomed to harsh words and blows; but words of kindness were strangers to his ears. For an hour he forgot the street and his uninviting home, and felt himself surrounded by a true home atmosphere. He almost fancied himself in his Calabrian home, with his mother and sisters about him—in his home as it was before cupidity entered his father's heart and impelled him to sell his own flesh and blood into slavery in a foreign land. Phil could not analyze his own emotions, but these were the feelings which rose in his heart, and filed it with transient sadness.

**A Calabrian village, like the one where
Phil and Giacomo are from.**

"I thank you much," he said. "I will come again some day."

"Come soon, Phil," said Paul. "You know where my necktie stand is. Come there any afternoon between four and five, and I will take you home to supper. Do you know the way out, or shall I go with you?"

"I know the way," said Phil.

He went downstairs and once more found himself on the sidewalk. It was but six o'clock, and five or six hours were still before him before he could feel at liberty to go home. Should he return too early, he would be punished for losing the possible gains of the hour he had lost, even if the sum he brought home were otherwise satisfactory. So, whatever may be his fatigue, or however inclement the weather, the poor Italian boy is compelled to stay out till near midnight, before he is permitted to return to the hard pallet on which only he can sleep off his fatigues.

Again in the street, Phil felt that he must make up for lost time. Now six o'clock is not a very favorable time for street music; citizens who do business downtown have mostly gone home to dinner. Those who have not started are in haste, and little disposed to heed the appeal of the young minstrel. Later the saloons will be well frequented, and not seldom the young fiddlers may pick up a few, sometimes a considerable number of pennies, by playing at the doors of these places, or within, if they should be invited to enter; but at six there is not much to be done.

After a little reflection, Phil determined to go down to Fulton Ferry and got on board the Brooklyn steamboat. He might get a chance to play to the passengers, and some, no doubt, would give him something. At any rate, the investment would be small, since for one fare, or two cents, he might ride back and forward several times, as long as he did not step off the boat. He, therefore, directed his steps toward the ferry, and arrived just in time to go on board the boat.

The boat was very full. So large a number of the people in Brooklyn are drawn to New York by business and pleasure, that the boats, particularly in the morning from seven to nine, and in the afternoon, from five to seven, go loaded down with foot passengers and carriages.

Phil entered the ladies' cabin. Though ostensibly confined to ladies' use, it was largely occupied also by gentlemen who did not enjoy the smoke which usually affects disagreeably the atmosphere of the cabin appropriated to their own sex. Our young musician knew that to children the hearts and purses of ladies are more likely to open than those of gentlemen, and this guided him.

Entering, he found every seat taken. He waited till the boat had started, and then, taking his position in the center of the rear cabin, he began to play and sing, fixing at once the attention of the passengers upon himself.

"That boy's a nuisance; he ought not to be allowed to play on the boat," muttered an old gentleman, looking up from the columns of the Evening Post.

"Now, papa," said a young lady at his side, "why need you object to the poor boy? I am sure he sings very nicely. I like to hear him."

"I don't."

"You know, papa, you have no taste for music. Why, you went to sleep at the opera the other evening."

"I tried to," said her father, in whom musical taste had a very limited development. "It was all nonsense to me."

"He is singing the Hymn of Garibaldi. What a sweet voice he has! Such a handsome little fellow, too!"

"He has a dirty face, and his clothes are quite ragged."

"But he has beautiful eyes; see how brilliant they are. No wonder he is dirty and ragged; it isn't his fault, poor boy. I have no doubt he has a miserable home. I'm going to give him something."

"Just as you like, Florence; as I am not a romantic young damsel, I shall not follow your example."'

By this time the song was finished, and Phil, taking off his cap, went the rounds. None of the contributions were larger than five cents, until he came to the young lady of whom we have spoken above. She drew a twenty-five-cent piece from her portemonnaie, and put it into Phil's hand, with a gracious smile, which pleased the young fiddler as much as the gift, welcome though that undoubtedly was.

"Thank you, lady," he said.

"You sing very nicely," she replied.

Phil smiled, and dirty though his face was, the smile lighted it up with rare beauty.

"Do you often come on these boats?" asked the young lady.

"Sometimes, but they do not always let me play," said Phil.

"I hope I shall hear you again. You have a good voice."

"Thank you, signorina."

"You can speak English. I tried to speak with one of you the other day, but he could only speak Italian."

"I know a few words, signorina."

"I hope I shall see you again," and the young lady, prompted by a natural impulse of kindness, held out her hand to the little musician. He took it respectfully, and bending over, touched it with his lips.

The young lady, to whom this was quite unexpected, smiled and blushed, by no means offended, but she glanced round her to see whether it was observed by others.

"Upon my word, Florence," said her father, as Phil moved away, "you have got up quite a scene with this little ragged musician. I am rather glad he is not ten or twelve years older, or there might be a romantic elopement."

"Now, papa, you are too bad," said Florence. "Just because I choose to be kind to a poor, neglected child, you fancy all sorts of improbable things."

"I don't know where you get all your foolish romance from—not from me, I am sure."

"I should think not," said Florence, laughing merrily. "Your worst enemy won't charge you with being romantic, papa."

"I hope not," said her father, shrugging his shoulders. "But the boat has touched the pier. Shall we go on shore, or have you any further business with your young Italian friend?"

"Not to-day, papa."

The passengers vacated the boat, and were replaced by a smaller number, on their way from Brooklyn to New York.

CHAPTER VI

THE BARROOM

Phil did not leave the boat. He lingered in the cabin until the passengers were seated, and after the boat was again under way began to play. This time, however, he was not as fortunate as before. While in the midst of a tune one of the men employed on the boat entered the cabin. At times he would not have interfered with him, but he happened to be in ill humor, and this proved unfortunate for Phil.

"Stop your noise, boy," he said.

Phil looked up.

"May I not play?"

"No; nobody wants to hear you."

The young fiddler did not dare to disobey. He saw that for the present his gains were at an end. However, he had enough to satisfy the rapacity of the padrone, and could afford to stop. He took a seat, and waited quietly till the boat landed. One of the lady passengers, as she passed him on her way out of the cabin, placed ten cents in his hand. This led him to count up his gains. He found they amounted to precisely two dollars and fifty cents.

"I need not play any more," he thought. "I shall not be beaten to-night."

He found his seat so comfortable, especially after wandering about the streets all day, that he remained on the boat for two more trips. Then, taking his violin under his arm, he went out on the pier.

It was half-past seven o'clock. He would like to have gone to his lodging, but knew that it would not be permitted. In this respect the Italian fiddler is not as well off as those who ply other street trades. Newsboys and bootblacks are their own masters, and, whether their earnings are little or great, reap the benefit of them themselves. They can stop work at six if they like, or earlier; but the little Italian musician must remain in the street till near midnight, and then, after a long and fatiguing day, he is liable to be beaten and sent to bed without his supper, unless he brings home a satisfactory sum of money.

Phil walked about here and there in the lower part of the city. As he was passing a barroom he was called in by the barkeeper.

"Give us a tune, boy," he said.

29

It was a low barroom, frequented by sailors and a rough set of customers of similar character. The red face of the barkeeper showed that he drank very liberally, and the atmosphere was filled with the fumes of bad cigars and bad liquor. The men were ready for a good time, as they called it, and it was at the suggestion of one of them that Phil had been invited in.

"Play a tune on your fiddle, you little ragamuffin," said one.

Phil cared little how he was addressed. He was at the service of the public, and what he chiefly cared for was that he be paid for his services.

"What shall I play?" he asked.

"Anything," hiccoughed one. "It's all the same to me. I don't know one tune from another."

The young fiddler played one of the popular airs of the day. He did not undertake to sing, for the atmosphere was so bad that he could hardly avoid coughing. He was anxious to get out into the street, but he did not wish to refuse playing. When he had finished his tune, one of those present, a sailor, cried, "That's good. Step up, boys, and have a drink."

The invitation was readily accepted by all except Phil. Noticing that the boy kept his place, the sailor said, "Step up, boy, and wet your whistle."

Phil liked the weak wines of his native land, but he did not care for the poisonous decoctions of be found in such places.

"I am not thirsty," he said.

"Yes, you are; here, give this boy a glass of brandy."

"I do not want it," said Phil.

"You won't drink with us," exclaimed the sailor, who had then enough to be quarrelsome. "Then I'll make you;" and he brought down his fist so heavily upon the counter as to make the glasses rattle. "Then I'll make you. Here, give me a glass, and I'll pour it down his throat."

The fiddler was frightened at his vehemence, and darted to the door. But the sailor was too quick for him. Overtaking Phil, he dragged him back with a rough grasp, and held out his hand for the glass. But an unexpected friend now turned up.

"Oh, let the boy go, Jack," said a fellow sailor. "If he don't want to drink, don't force him."

But his persecutor was made ugly by his potations, and swore that Phil should drink before he left the barroom.

"That he shall not," said his new friend.

"Who is to prevent it?" demanded Jack, fiercely.

"I will."

"Then I'll pour a glass down your throat, too," returned Jack, menacingly.

"No need of that. I am ready enough to drink. But the boy shan't drink, if he don't want to."

"He shall!" retorted the first sailor, with an oath.

Still holding Phil by the shoulder with one hand, with the other he took a glass which had just been filled with brandy; he was about to pour it down his throat, when the glass was suddenly dashed from his hand and broke upon the floor.

With a fresh oath Jack released his hold on Phil, and, maddened with rage, threw himself upon the other. Instantly there was a general melee. Phil did not wait to see the result. He ran to the door, and, emerging into the street, ran away till he had placed a considerable distance between himself and the disorderly and drunken party in the barroom. The fight there continued until the police, attracted by the noise, forced an entrance and carried away the whole party to the station-house, where they had a chance to sleep off their potations.

Freed from immediate danger, the young fiddler kept on his way. He had witnessed such scenes before, as he had often been into barrooms to play in the evening. He had not been paid for his trouble, but he cared little for that, as the money would have done him no good. He would only have been compelled to pass it over to the padrone. These boys, even at a tender age, are necessarily made familiar with the darker side of metropolitan life. Vice and crime are displayed before their young eyes, and if they do not themselves become vicious, it is not for the want of knowledge and example.

It would be tedious to follow Phil in his wanderings. We have already had a glimpse of the manner in which the days passed with him; only it is to be said that this was a favorable specimen. He had been more fortunate in collecting money than usual. Besides, he had had a better dinner than usual, thanks to the apple, and a supper such as he had not tasted for months.

About ten o'clock, as he was walking on the Bowery, he met Giacomo, his companion of the morning.

The little boy was dragging one foot after the other wearily. There was a sad look on his young face, for he had not been successful, and he knew too well how he would be received by the padrone. Yet his face lighted up as he saw Phil. Often before Phil had encouraged him when he was despondent. He looked upon our young hero as his only friend; for there was no other of the boys who seemed to care for him or able to help him.

"Is it you, Filippo?" he said.

"Yes, Giacomo. What luck have you had?"

"Not much. I have only a little more than a dollar. I am so tired; but I don't dare go back. The padrone will beat me."

An idea came to Phil. He did not know how much money he had; but he was sure it must be considerably more than two dollars, Why should he not give some to his friend to make up his deficiencies, and so perhaps save him from punishment?

"I have had better luck," he said. "I have almost three dollars."

"You are always luckier than I, Filippo."

"I am stronger, Giacomo. It does not tire me so much to walk about."

"You can sing, too. I cannot sing very much, and I do not get so much money."

"Tell me just how much money you have, Giacomo."

"I have a dollar and thirty cents," said Giacomo, after counting the contents of his pockets.

Meanwhile Phil had been doing the same thing. The result of his count was that he found he had two dollars and eighty cents.

"Listen, Giacomo," he said. "I will give you enough to make two dollars."

"But then you will be beaten."

"No; I shall have two dollars and five cents left. Then neither of us will get beaten."

"How kind you are, Filippo!"

"Oh, it is nothing. Besides, I do not want to carry too much, or the padrone will expect me to bring as much every day, and that I cannot do. So it will be better for us both."

The transfer was quickly made, and the two boys kept together until they heard the clock strike eleven. It was now so late that they determined to return to their miserable lodging, for both were tired and longed for sleep.

CHAPTER VII

THE HOME OF THE BOYS

It was a quarter-past eleven when Phil and Giacomo entered the shabby brick house which they called home, for want of a better. From fifteen to twenty of their companions had already arrived, and the padrone was occupied in receiving their several contributions. The apartment was a mean one, miserably furnished, but seemed befitting the principal occupant, whose dark face was marked by an expression of greed, and alternately showed satisfaction or disappointment as the contents of the boys' pockets were satisfactory or otherwise. Those who had done badly were set apart for punishment.

He looked up as the two boys entered.

"Well, Filippo," he said, harshly, "how much have you got?"

Phil handed over his earnings. They were up to the required limit, but the padrone looked only half satisfied.

"Is that all you have?" he asked, suspiciously.

"It is all, signore."

"You have not done well this afternoon, then. When I met you at twelve o'clock you had more than a dollar."

"It was because a good signora gave me fifty cents."

The padrone, still suspicious, plunging his hands into Phil's pockets, but in vain. He could not find another penny.

"Take off your shoes and stockings," he said, still unsatisfied.

Phil obediently removed his shoes and stockings, but no money was found concealed, as the padrone half suspected. Sometimes these poor boys, beset by a natural temptation, secrete a portion of their daily earnings. Whenever they are detected, woe betide them. The padrone makes an example of them, inflicting a cruel punishment, in order to deter other boys from imitating them.

Having discovered nothing, he took Phil's violin, and proceeded to Giacomo.

"Now for you," he said.

Giacomo handed over his money. The padrone was surprised in turn, but his surprise was of a different nature. He had expected to find him deficient, knowing that he was less enterprising than Phil. He was glad to get more money than he expected, but a little disappointed that he had no good excuse for beating him; for he had one of those hard, cruel natures that delight in inflicting pain and anguish upon others.

"Take care that you do as well to-morrow," he said. "Go and get your supper."

One of the larger boys was distributing bread and cheese to the hungry boys. Nearly all ate as if famished, plain and uninviting as was the supper, for they had been many hours without food. But Phil, who, as we know, had eaten a good supper at Mrs. Hoffman's, felt very little appetite. He slyly gave his bread to one of the boys, who, on account of the small sum he brought home, had been sentenced to go without. But the sharp eyes of the padrone, which, despite his occupation, managed to see all that was going on, detected this action, and he became suspicious that Phil had bought supper out of his earnings.

"Why did you give your bread to Giuseppe?" he demanded.

"Because I was not hungry," answered Phil.

"Why were you not hungry? Did you buy some supper?"

"No, signore."

"Then you should be hungry."

"A kind lady gave me some supper."

"How did it happen?"

"I knew her son. His name is Paolo. He asked me to go home with him. Then he gave me a good supper."

"How long were you there? You might have been playing and brought me some more money," said the padrone, who, with characteristic meanness, grudged the young fiddler time to eat the meal that cost him nothing.

"It was not long, signore."

"You can eat what is given you, but you must not waste too much time."

A boy entered next, who showed by his hesitating manner that he did not anticipate a good reception. The padrone, accustomed to judge by appearances, instantly divined this.

"Well, Ludovico," he said, sharply, "what do you bring me?"

"Pardon, padrone," said Ludovico, producing a small sum of money.

"I could not help it."

"Seventy-five cents," repeated the padrone, indignantly. "You have been idle, you little wretch!"

"No, padrone. Indeed, I did my best. The people would not give me money."

"Where did you go?"

"I was in Brooklyn."

"You have spent some of the money."

"No, padrone."

"You have been idle, then. No supper to-night. Pietro, my stick!"

Pietro was one of the older boys. He was ugly physically, and his disposition corresponded with his appearance. He could have few good traits, or he would not have possessed the confidence of the padrone. He was an efficient assistant of the latter, and co-operated with him in oppressing the other boys. Indeed, he was a nephew of the padrone's, and for this reason, as well as his similarity of disposition, he was treated with unusual indulgence. Whenever the padrone felt suspicious of any of the boys, he usually sent them out in company with Pietro, who acted as a spy, faithfully reporting all that happened to his principal.

Pietro responded with alacrity to the command of the padrone, and produced a stout stick, which he handed to his uncle.

"Now strip off your jacket," said the padrone, harshly.

"Spare me, padrone! Do not beat me! It was not my fault," said the unhappy Ludovico, imploringly.

"Take off your jacket!" repeated the padrone, pitilessly.

One look of that hard face might have taught Ludovico, even if he had not witnessed the punishment so often inflicted on other boys, that there was no hope for him.

"Help him, Pietro," said the padrone.

Pietro seized Ludovico's jacket, and pulled it off roughly. Then he drew off the ragged shirt which the boy wore underneath, and his bare back was exposed to view.

"Hold him, Pietro!"

In Pietro's firm grasp, the boy was unable to stir. The padrone whirled the stick aloft, and brought it down upon the naked flesh, leaving behind a fearful wheal.

Ludovico shrieked aloud, and again implored mercy, but in vain, for the stick descended again and again.

Meanwhile the other boys looked on, helpless to interfere. The more selfish were glad that they had escaped, though not at all sure but it would be their turn next evening. There were others who felt a

---

passive sympathy for their unlucky comrade. Others were filled with indignation at the padrone, knowing how cruel and unjust were his exactions. Among these was Phil. Possessed of a warm and sympathetic heart, he never witnessed these cruel punishments without feeling that he would like to see the padrone suffering such pain as he inflicted upon others.

"If I were only a man," he often thought, "I would wrench the stick from his hand, and give him a chance to feel it."

But he knew too well the danger of permitting his real sentiments to be reflected in his face. It would only bring upon him a share of the same punishment, without benefiting those who were unfortunate enough to receive it.

When Ludovico's punishment was ended, he was permitted to go to bed, but without his supper. Nor was his the only case. Five other boys were subjected to the same punishment. The stick had no want of exercise on that evening. Here were nearly forty boys, subjected to excessive fatigue, privation, and brutal treatment daily, on account of the greed of one man. The hours that should been given in part to instruction, and partly to such recreation as the youthful heart craves, were devoted to a pursuit that did nothing to prepare them for the duties of life. And this white slavery—for it merits no better name—is permitted by the law of two great nations. Italy is in fault in suffering this traffic in her children of tender years, and America is guilty as well in not interfering, as she might, at all events, to abridge the long hours of labor required of these boys, and forcing their cruel guardians to give them some instruction.

One by one the boys straggled in. By midnight all had returned, and the boys were permitted to retire to their beds, which were poor enough. This, however, was the least of their troubles. Sound are the slumbers of young however hard the couch on which it rests, especially when, as with all the young Italian boys, the day has been one of fatigue.

CHAPTER VIII
A COLD DAY

The events thus far recorded in the life of our young hero took place on a day toward the middle of October, when the temperature was sufficiently mild to produce no particular discomfort in those exposed to it. We advance our story two months, and behold Phil setting out for his day's wandering on a morning in December, when the keen blasts swept through the streets, sending a shiver through the frames even of those who were well protected. How much more, then, must it be felt by the young street musician, who, with the exception of a woolen tippet, wore nothing more or warmer than in the warmer months! Yet, Phil, with his natural vigorous frame, was better able to bear the rigor of the winter weather than some of his comrades, as Giacomo, to whom the long hours spent in the streets were laden with suffering and misery.

The two boys went about together when they dared to do so, though the padrone objected, but for what reason it did not seem manifest, unless because he suspected that two would plan something prejudicial to his interests. Phil, who was generally more successful than Giacomo, often made up his smaller comrade's deficiencies by giving him a portion of his own gains.

It was a raw day. Only those who felt absolutely obliged to be out were to be seen in the streets; but among these were our two little fiddlers. Whatever might be the weather, they were compelled to expose themselves to its severity. However the boys might suffer, they must bring home the usual amount. But at eleven o'clock the prospects seemed rather discouraging. They had but twenty-five cents between them, nor would anyone stop to listen to their playing.

"I wish it were night, Filippo," said Giacomo, shivering with cold.

"So do I, Giacomo. Are you very cold?"

"Yes," said the little boy, his teeth chattering. "I wish I were back in Italy. It is never so cold there."

"No, Giacomo; you are right. But I would not mind the cold so much, if I had a warm overcoat like that boy," pointing out a boy clad in a thick overcoat, and a fur cap drawn over his ears, while his hands were snugly incased in warm gloves.

He, too, looked at the two fiddlers, and he could not help noticing how cold they looked.

"Look here, you little chaps, are you cold? You look as if you had just come from Greenland."

"Yes," said Phil. "We are cold."

"Your hands look red enough. Here is an old pair of gloves for one of you. I wish I had another pair. They are not very thick, but they are better than none."

He drew a pair of worsted gloves from his pocket, and handed them to Phil.

"Thank you," said Phil; but having received them, he gave them to Giacomo.

"You are colder than I am, Giacomo," he said. "Take them."

"But you are cold, too, Filippo."

"I will put my hands in my pockets. Don't mind me."

Of course this conversation took place in Italian; for, though Phil had learned considerable English, Giacomo understood but a few words of it.

The gloves afforded some protection, but still both boys were very cold. They were in Brooklyn, having crossed the ferry in the morning. They had wandered to a part not closely built up, where they were less sheltered, and experienced greater discomfort.

"Can't we go in somewhere and get warm? pleaded Giacomo.

"Here is a grocery store. We will go in there."

Phil opened the door and entered. The shopkeeper, a peevish-looking man, with lightish hair, stood behind the counter weighing out a pound of tea for a customer.

"What do you want here, you little vagabonds?" he exclaimed, harshly, as he saw the two boys enter.

"We are cold," said Phil. "May we stand by your stove and get warm?"

"Do you think I provide a fire for all the vagabonds in the city?" said the grocer, with a brutal disregard of their evident suffering.

Phil hesitated, not knowing whether he was ordered out or not.

"Clear out of my store, I say!" said the grocer, harshly. "I don't want you in here. Do you understand?"

At this moment a gentleman of prepossessing appearance entered the store. He heard the grocer's last words, and their inhumanity made him indignant.

"What do these boys want, Mr. Perkins?" he said.

"They want to spend their time in my shop. I have no room for such vagabonds."

"We are cold," said Phil. "We only want to warm ourselves by the fire."

"I don't want you here," said the grocer, irritably.

"Mr. Perkins," said the gentleman, sharply, "have you no humanity? What harm can it do you to let these poor boys get warm by your fire? It will cost you nothing; it will not diminish your personal comfort; yet you drive them out into the cold."

The grocer began to perceive that he was on the wrong tack. The gentleman who addressed him was a regular and profitable customer, and he did not like to incur his ill will, which would entail loss.

"They can stay, Mr. Pomeroy," he said, with an ill grace, "since you ask it."

"I do not ask it. I will not accept, as a personal favor, what you should have granted from a motive of humanity, more especially as, after this exhibition of your spirit, I shall not trade here any longer."

By this time the grocer perceived that he had made a mistake.

"I hope you will reconsider that, Mr. Pomeroy," he said, abjectly. "The fact is, I had no objections to the boys warming themselves, but they are mostly thieves, and I could not keep my eyes on them all the time."

"I think you are mistaken. They don't look like thieves. Did you ever have anything stolen by one of this class of boys?"

"Not that I know of," said the grocer, hesitatingly; "but it is likely they would steal if they got a chance."

"We have no right to say that of anyone without good cause."

"We never steal," said Phil, indignantly; for he understood what was said.

"Of course he says so," sneered the grocer. "Come and warm yourselves, if you want to."

The boys accepted this grudging invitation, and drew near the stove. They spread out their hands, and returning warmth proved very grateful to them.

"Have you been out long?" asked the gentleman who had interceded in their behalf, also drawing near the stove.

"Since eight, signore."

"Do you live in Brooklyn?"

"No; in New York."

"And do you go out every day?"

"Si, signore."

"How long since you came from Italy?"

"A year."

"Would you like to go back?"

"He would," said Phil, pointing to his companion. "I would like to stay here, if I had a good home."

"What kind of a home have you? With whom do you live?"

"With the padrone."

"I suppose that means your guardian?"

"Yes, sir," answered Phil.

"Is he kind to you?"

"He beats us if we do not bring home enough money."

"Your lot is a hard one. What makes you stay with him? Don't the boys ever run away?"

"Sometimes."

"What does the padrone do in that case?"

"He tries to find them."

"And if he does—what then?"

"He beats them for a long time."

"Evidently your padrone is a brute. Why don't you complain to the police?"

Phil shrugged his shoulders, and did not answer. He evidently thought the suggestion an impracticable one. These boys are wont to regard the padrone as above all law. His power seems to them absolute, and they never dream of any interference. And, indeed, there is some reason for their cherishing this opinion. However brutal his treatment, I know of no case where the law has stepped in to rescue the young victim. This is partly, no doubt, because the boys, few of whom can speak the English language, do not know their rights, and seldom complain to outsiders—never to the authorities. Probably, in some cases, the treatment is less brutal than I have depicted; but from the best information I can obtain from trustworthy sources, I fear that the reality, if anything, exceeds the picture I have drawn.

"I think I should enjoy giving your padrone a horsewhipping," said the gentleman, impetuously. "Can such things be permitted in the nineteenth century?"

40

"I have no doubt the little rascals deserve all they get," said the grocer, who would probably have found in the Italian padrone a congenial spirit.

Mr. Pomeroy deigned no reply to this remark.

"Well, boys," he said, consulting his watch, "I must leave you. Here are twenty-five cents for each of you. I have one piece of advice for you. If your padrone beats you badly, run away from him. I would if I were in your place."

"Addio, signore," said the two boys.

"I suppose that means 'good-by.' Well, good-by, and better luck."

CHAPTER IX

PIETRO THE SPY

Though from motives of policy the grocer had permitted the boys to warm themselves by his fire, he felt only the more incensed against them on this account, and when Mr. Pomeroy had gone determined to get rid of them.

"Haven't you got warm yet?" he asked. "I can't have you in my way all day."

"We will go," said Phil. "Come, Giacomo."

He did not thank the grocer, knowing how grudgingly permission had been given.

So they went out again into the chill air, but they had got thoroughly warmed, and were better able to bear it.

"Where shall we go, Filippo?" asked the younger boy.

"We will go back to New York. It is not so cold there."

Giacomo unhesitatingly assented to whatever Phil proposed. He was not self-reliant, like our hero, but always liked to have someone to lean upon.

They made their way back to Fulton Ferry in a leisurely manner, stopping here and there to play; but it was a bad day for business. The cold was such that no one stopped to give them anything, except that one young man dropped ten cents in Phil's hand as he hurried by, on his way home.

At length they reached the ferry. The passengers were not so many in number as usual. The cabin was so warm and comfortable that they remained on board for two or three trips, playing each time. In this way they obtained about thirty cents more. They would have remained longer, but that one of the deck hands asked, "How many times are you going across for two cents?" and this made them think it prudent to go.

When six o'clock came Giacomo asked Phil, who acted as treasurer, how much money they had.

"Two dollars," answered Phil.

"That is only one dollar for each."

"Yes, Giacomo."

"Then we shall be beaten," said the little boy, with a sigh.

"I am afraid so."

"And get no supper."

"Yes," said Phil; "unless," he added, "we get some supper now."

"With this money?" asked Giacomo, startled at the boldness of the suggestion.

"Yes; we shall be beaten at any rate. It will be no worse for us if we get some supper."

"Will you buy some bread?"

"No," said Phil, daringly. "I am going to buy some meat."

"What will the padrone say?"

"I shall not tell the padrone."

"Do you think he will find out?"

"No. Besides, we ought to have some supper after walking about all day."

Evidently Phil had begun to think, and the essential injustice of laboring without proper compensation had impressed his youthful mind. Giacomo was more timid. He had not advanced as far as Phil, nor was he as daring. But I have already said that he was guided in a great measure by Phil, and so it proved in this case.

Phil, having made up his mind, set about carrying his plan into execution. Only a block distant was a cheap restaurant, where plates of meat were supplied to a poor class of customers at ten cents per plate.

"Let us go in here," he said.

Giacomo followed, but not without trepidation. He knew that what they were about to do would be a heinous crime in the eyes of the padrone. Even Phil had never ventured upon such direct rebellion before. But Mr. Pomeroy's suggestion that he should run away was beginning to bear fruit in his mind. He had not come to that yet, but he might. Why should he not earn money for his own benefit, as well as for the padrone? True, he was bound to the latter by a legal contract entered into by his father, but Phil, without knowing much about law, had an indistinct idea that the contract was a one-sided one, and was wholly for the advantage of the other party. The tyrant is always in danger of losing his hold upon the victim when the latter begins to think.

They entered the restaurant, and sat down at a table.

The tables were greasy. The floor was strewed with sawdust. The waiters were dirty, and the entire establishment was neither neat nor inviting. But it was democratic. No customers were sent away because they were unfashionably attired. The only requisite was money enough to defray their bills. Nevertheless Giacomo felt a

---

little in awe even of the dirty waiters. His frugal meals were usually bought at the baker's shop, and eaten standing in the street. Sitting down at a table, even though it was greasy, seemed a degree of luxury to which he was not entitled. But Phil more easily adapted himself to circumstances. He knew that he had as much right there as any other customer.

Presently a waiter presented himself.

"Have you ordered?" he asked.

"Give me some roast beef," said Phil. "What will you have, Giacomo?"

"The same as you, Filippo," said Giacomo, in Italian.

"What's that?" asked the waiter, thinking he had named some dish.

"He will have some roast beef, too. Will you have some coffee, Giacomo?"

"If you have it," answered the smaller boy.

So Phil gave the double order, and very soon the coffee and meat were placed before them. I suspect that few of my readers would have regarded these articles with any relish. One need not be fastidious to find fault with the dark-hued beverage, which was only a poor imitation of coffee, and the dark fragments of meat, which might have been horseflesh so far as appearance went. But to the two Italian boys it was indeed a feast. The coffee, which was hot, warmed their stomachs, and seemed to them like nectar, while the meat was as palatable as the epicure finds his choicest dishes. While eating, even Giacomo forgot that he was engaged in something unlawful, and his face was lighted up with rare satisfaction.

"It is good," said Phil, briefly, as he laid down his knife and fork, after disposing of the last morsel upon his plate.

"I wish I could have such a supper every day," said Giacomo.

"I will when I am a man," said Phil.

"I don't think I shall ever be a man," said Giacomo, shaking his head.

"Why not?" asked Phil, regarding him with surprise.

"I do not think I shall live."

"What makes you think so, Giacomo?" said Phil, startled.

"I am not strong, Filippo," said the little boy, "I think I get weaker every day. I long so much to go back to Italy. If I could see my mother once more, I would be willing to die then."

"You must not think of such things, Giacomo," said Phil, who, like most healthy boys, did not like to think of death. "You will get strong when summer comes. The weather is bad now, of course."

"I don't think I shall, Filippo. Do you remember Matteo?"

"Yes, I remember him."

Matteo was a comrade who had died six months before. He was a young boy, about the size and age of Giacomo.

"I dreamed of him last night, Filippo. He held out his hand to me."

"Well?"

"I think I am going to die, like him."

"Don't be foolish, Giacomo," said Phil. But, though he said this, even he was startled by what Giacomo had told him. He was ignorant, and the ignorant are prone to superstition; so he felt uncomfortable, but did not like to acknowledge it.

"You must not think of this, Giacomo," he said. "You will be an old man some day."

"That's for you, Filippo. It isn't for me," said the little boy.

"Come, let us go," said Phil, desirous of dropping the subject.

He went up to the desk, and paid for both, the sum of thirty cents.

"Now, come," he said.

Giacomo followed him out, and they turned down the street, feeling refreshed by the supper they had eaten. But unfortunately they had been observed. As they left the restaurant, they attracted the attention of Pietro, whom chance had brought thither at an unfortunate time. His sinister face lighted up with joy as he realized the discovery he had made. But he wished to make sure that it was as he supposed. They might have gone in only to play and sing.

He crossed the street, unobserved by Phil and Giacomo, and entered the restaurant.

"Were my two brothers here?" he asked, assuming relationship.

"Two boys with fiddles?"

"Yes; they just went out."

"Did they get supper?"

"Yes; they had some roast beef and coffee."

"Thank you," said Pietro, and he left the restaurant with his suspicions confirmed.

"I shall tell the padrone," he said to himself.

"They will feel the stick to-night."

CHAPTER X

FRENCH'S HOTEL

Pietro had one of those mean and malignant natures that are best pleased when they are instrumental in bringing others into trouble. He looked forward to becoming a padrone himself some time, and seemed admirably fitted by nature to exercise the inhuman office. He lost no time, on his return, in making known to his uncle what he had learned.

For the boys to appropriate to their own use money which had been received for their services was, in the eyes of the padrone, a crime of the darkest shade. In fact, if the example were generally followed, it would have made a large diminution of his income, though the boys might have been benefited. He listened to Pietro with an ominous scowl, and decided to inflict condign punishment upon the young offenders.

Meanwhile Phil and Giacomo resumed their wanderings. They no longer hoped to make up the large difference between what they had and the sum they were expected by the padrone to bring. As the evening advanced the cold increased, and penetrated through their thin clothing, chilling them through and through. Giacomo felt it the most. By and by he began to sob with the cold and fatigue.

"What is the matter, Giacomo?" asked Phil, anxiously.

"I feel so cold, Filippo—so cold and tired. I wish I could rest."

The boys were in Printing House Square, near the spot where now stands the Franklin statue.

After the boys eat lunch, and decide that they're going to be beaten anyway, they go into a hotel on Printing House Square to get warm.

"If you want to rest, Giacomo," said Phil, pityingly, "we will go into French's Hotel a little while."

"I should like to."

They entered the hotel and sat down near the heater. The grateful warmth diffused itself through their frames, and Giacomo sank back in his seat with a sigh of relief.

"Do you feel better, Giacomo?" asked his comrade.

"Yes, Filippo; I wish I could stay here till it is time to go home."

"We will, then. We shall get no more money outside."

"The padrone——"

"Will beat us at any rate. It will be no worse for us. Besides they may possibly ask us to play here."

"I can play no more to-night, Filippo, I am so tired."

Phil knew very little of sickness, or he might have seen that Giacomo was going to be ill. Exposure, fatigue, and privation had been too much for his strength. He had never been robust, and he had been subjected to trials that would have proved hard for one much stronger to bear.

When he had once determined to remain in the comfortable hotel, Phil leaned back in his chair also, and decided to enjoy all the comfort attainable. What though there was a beating in prospect?

He had before him two or three hours of rest and relief from the outside cold. He was something of a philosopher, and chose not to let future evil interfere with present good.

47

Near the two boys sat two young men—merchants from the interior of New York State, who were making a business visit to the metropolis.

"Well, Gardner," said the first, "where shall we go to-night?"

"Why need we go anywhere?"

"I thought you might like to go to some place of amusement."

"So I would if the weather were less inclement. The most comfortable place is by the fire."

"You are right as to that, but the evening will be long and stupid."

"Oh, we can worry it through. Here, for instance, are two young musicians," indicating the little fiddlers. "Suppose we get a tune out of them?"

"Agreed. Here, boy, can you play on that fiddle?"

"Yes," said Phil.

"Well, give us a tune, then. Is that your brother?"

"No, he is my comrade."

"He can play, too."

"Will you play, Giacomo?"

The younger boy roused himself. The two stood up, and played two or three tunes successfully. A group of loungers gathered around them and listened approvingly. When they had finished Phil took off his hat and went the rounds. Some gave, the two first mentioned contributing most liberally. The whole sum collected was about fifty cents.

Phil and Giacomo now resumed their seats. They felt now that they were entitled to rest for the remainder of the evening, since they had gained quite as much as they would have been likely to earn in wandering about the streets. The group that had gathered about them dispersed, and they ceased to be objects of attention. Fatigue and the warmth of the room gradually affected Giacomo until he leaned back and fell asleep.

"I won't take him till it's time to go back," thought Phil.

So Giacomo slept on, despite the noises in the street outside and the confusion incident to every large hotel. As he sat asleep, he attracted the attention of a stout gentleman who was passing, leading by the hand a boy of ten.

"Is that your brother?" he asked in a low tone of Phil.

"No, signore; it is my comrade."

"So you go about together?"

"Yes, sir," answered Phil, bethinking himself to use English instead of Italian.

"He seems tired."

"Yes; he is not so strong as I am."

"Do you play about the streets all day?"

"Yes, sir."

"How would you like that, Henry?" asked his father to the boy at his side.

"I should like to play about the streets all day," said Henry, roguishly, misinterpreting the word "play."

"I think you would get tired of it. What is your name, my boy?"

"Filippo."

"And what is the name of your friend?"

"Giacomo."

"Did you never go to school?"

Phil shook his head.

"Would you like to go?"

"Yes, sir."

"You would like it better than wandering about the streets all day?"

"Yes, sir."

"Why do you not ask your father to send you to school?"

"My father is in Italy."

"And his father, also?"

"Si, signore," answered Phil, relapsing into Italian.

"What do you think of that, Henry?" asked the gentleman. "How should you like to leave me, and go to some Italian city to roam about all day, playing on the violin?"

"I think I would rather go to school."

"I think you would."

"Are you often out so late, Filippo? I think that is the name you gave me."

Phil shrugged his shoulders.

"Always," he answered.

"At what time do you go home?"

"At eleven."

"It is too late for a boy of your age to sit up. Why do you not go home sooner?"

"The padrone would beat me."

Who is the padrone?"

"The man who brought me from Italy to America."

"Poor boys!" said the gentleman, compassionately. "Yours is a hard life. I hope some time you will be in a better position."

Phil fixed his dark eyes upon the stranger, grateful for his words of sympathy.

"Thank you," he said.

"Good-night," said the stranger, kindly.

"Good-night, signore."

An hour passed. The City Hall clock near by struck eleven. The time had come for returning to their mercenary guardian. Phil shook the sleeping form of Giacomo. The little boy stirred in his sleep, and murmured, "Madre." He had been dreaming of his mother and his far-off Italian home. He woke to the harsh realities of life, four thousand miles away from that mother and home.

"Have I slept, Filippo?" he asked, rubbing his eyes, and looking about him in momentary bewilderment.

"Yes, Giacomo. You have slept for two hours and more. It is eleven o'clock."

"Then we must go back."

"Yes; take your violin, and we will go."

They passed out into the cold street, which seemed yet colder by contrast with the warm hotel they just left, and, crossing to the sidewalk that skirts the park, walked up Centre street.

Giacomo was seized with a fit of trembling. His teeth chattered with the cold. A fever was approaching, although neither he nor his companion knew it.

"Are you cold, Giacomo?" asked Phil, noticing how he trembled.

"I am very cold. I feel sick, Filippo."

"You will feel better to-morrow," said Phil; but the thought of the beating which his little comrade was sure to receive saddened him more than the prospect of being treated in the same way himself.

They kept on their way, past the Tombs with its gloomy entrance, through the ill-lighted street, scarcely noticed by the policeman whom they passed—for he was accustomed to see boys of their class out late at night—until at last they reached the dwelling of the padrone, who was waiting their arrival with the eagerness of a brutal nature, impatient to inflict pain.

CHAPTER XI

THE BOYS RECEPTION

Phil and Giacomo entered the lodging-house, wholly unconscious of the threatening storm, The padrone scowled at them as they entered but that was nothing unusual. Had he greeted them kindly, they would have had reason to be surprised.

"Well," he said, harshly, "how much do you bring?"

The boys produced two dollars and a half which he pocketed.

"Is this all?" he asked.

"It was cold," said Phil, "and we could not get more."

The padrone listened with an ominous frown.

"Are you hungry?" he asked. "Do you want your supper?"

Phil was puzzled by his manner, for he expected to be deprived of his supper on account of bringing less money than usual. Why should the padrone ask him if he wanted his supper? Though he was not hungry, he thought it best to answer in the affirmative.

"What would you like?" asked the padrone.

Again Phil was puzzled, for the suppers supplied by the padrone never varied, always consisting of bread and cheese.

"Perhaps," continued the padrone, meeting no answer, "you would like to have coffee and roast beef."

All was clear now. Phil understood that he had been seen going in or out of the restaurant, though he could not tell by whom. He knew well enough what to expect, but a chivalrous feeling of friendship led him to try to shield his young companion, even at the risk of a more severe punishment to be inflicted upon himself.

"It was my fault," he said, manfully. "Giacomo would not have gone in but for me."

"Wicked, ungrateful boy!" exclaimed the padrone, wrathfully. "It was my money that you spent. You are a thief!"

Phil felt that this was a hard word, which he did not deserve. The money was earned by himself, though claimed by the padrone. But he did not venture to say this. It would have been revolutionary. He thought it prudent to be silent.

"Why do you say nothing?" exclaimed the padrone, stamping his foot. "Why did you spend my money?"

"I was hungry."

"So you must live like a nobleman! Our supper is not good enough for you. How much did you spend?"

"Thirty cents."

"For each?"

"No, signore, for both."

"Then you shall have each fifteen blows, one for each penny. I will teach you to be a thief. Pietro, the stick! Now, strip!"

"Padrone," said Phil, generously, "let me have all the blows. It was my fault; Giacomo only went because I asked him."

If the padrone had had a heart, this generous request would have touched it; but he was not troubled in that way.

"He must be whipped, too," he said. "He should not have gone with you."

"He is sick, padrone," persisted Phil. "Excuse him till he is better."

"Not a word more," roared the padrone, irritated at his persistence. "If he is sick, it is because he has eaten too much," he added, with a sneer. "Pietro, my stick!"

The two boys began to strip mechanically, knowing that there was no appeal. Phil stood bare to the waist. The padrone seized the stick and began to belabor him. Phil's brown face showed by its contortions the pain he suffered, but he was too proud to cry out. When the punishment was finished his back was streaked with red, and looked maimed and bruised.

"Put on your shirt!" commanded the tyrant.

Phil drew it on over his bleeding back and resumed his place among his comrades.

"Now!" said the padrone, beckoning to Giacomo.

The little boy approached shivering, not so much with cold as with the fever that had already begun to prey upon him.

Phil turned pale and sick as he looked at the padrone preparing to inflict punishment. He would gladly have left the room, but he knew that it would not be permitted.

The first blow descended heavily upon the shrinking form of the little victim. It was followed by a shriek of pain and terror.

"What are you howling at?" muttered the padrone, between his teeth. "I will whip you the harder."

Giacomo would have been less able to bear the cruel punishment than Phil if he had been well, but being sick, it was all the more terrible to him. The second blow likewise was followed by a shriek of anguish. Phil looked on with pale face, set teeth, and blazing eyes, as he saw the barbarous punishment of his comrade. He felt that he hated the padrone with a fierce hatred. Had his strength been equal to the attempt, he would have flung himself upon the padrone. As it was, he looked at his comrades, half wishing that they would combine with him against their joint oppressor. But there was no hope of that. Some congratulated themselves that they were not in Giacomo's place; others looked upon his punishment as a matter of course. There was no dream of interference, save in the mind of Phil.

The punishment continued amid the groans and prayers for mercy of the little sufferer. But at the eighth stroke his pain and terror reached a climax, and nature succumbed. He sank on the floor, fainting. The padrone thought at first it was a pretense, and was about to repeat the strokes, when a look at the pallid, colorless face of the little sufferer alarmed him. It did not excite his compassion, but kindled the fear that the boy might be dying, in which case the police might interfere and give him trouble; therefore he desisted, but unwillingly.

"He is sick," said Phil, starting forward.

"He is no more sick than I am," scowled the padrone. "Pietro, some water!"

Pietro brought a glass of water, which the padrone threw in the face of the fallen boy. The shock brought him partial to. He opened his eyes, and looked around vacantly.

"What is the matter with you?" demanded the padrone, harshly.

"Where am I?" asked Giacomo, bewildered. But, as he asked this question, his eyes met the dark look of his tyrant, and he clasped his hands in terror.

"Do not beat me!" he pleaded. "I feel sick."

"He is only shamming," said Pietro, who was worthy to be the servant and nephew of such a master. But the padrone thought it would not be prudent to continue the punishment.

"Help him put on his clothes, Pietro," he said. "I will let you off this time, little rascal, but take heed that you never again steal a single cent of my money."

Giacomo was allowed to seek his uncomfortable bed. His back was so sore with the beating he had received that he was compelled to lie on his side. During the night the feverish symptoms increased, and before morning he was very sick. The padrone was forced to

---

take some measures for his recovery, not from motives of humanity, but because Giacomo's death would cut off a source of daily revenue, and this, in the eyes of the mercenary padrone, was an important consideration.

Phil went to bed in silence. Though he was suffering from the brutal blows he had received, the thought of the punishment and suffering of Giacomo affected him more deeply than his own. As I have said, the two boys came from the same town in southern Italy. They had known each other almost from infancy, and something of a fraternal feeling had grown up between them. In Phil's case, since he was the stronger, it was accompanied by the feeling that he should be a protector to the younger boy, who, on his side, looked up to Phil as stronger and wiser than himself. Though only a boy of twelve, what had happened led Phil to think seriously of his position and prospects. He did not know for how long his services had been sold to the padrone by his father, but he felt sure that the letter of the contract would be little regarded as long as his services were found profitable.

What hope, then, had he of better treatment in the future? There seemed no prospect except of continued oppression and long days of hardship, unless—and here the suggestion of Mr. Pomeroy occurred to him—unless he ran away. He had known of boys doing this before. Some had been brought back, and, of course, were punished severely for their temerity, but others had escaped, and had never returned. What had become of them Phil did not know, but he rightly concluded that they could not be any worse off than in the service of the padrone. Thinking of all this, Phil began to think it probable that he, too, would some day break his bonds and run away. He did not fix upon any time. He had not got as far as this. But circumstances, as we shall find in our next chapter, hastened his determination, and this, though he knew it not, was the last night he would sleep in the house of the padrone.

CHAPTER XII

GIACOMO'S PRESENTIMENTS

Phil woke up the next morning feeling lame and sore. His back bore traces of the flogging he had received the night before. As his eyes opened, they rested upon twenty boys lying about him, and also upon the dark, unsightly walls of the shabby room, and the prospect before him served to depress even his hopeful temperament. But he was not permitted to meditate long. Pietro opened the door, and called out in harsh tones: "Get up, all of you, or the padrone will be here with his stick!"

The invitation was heard and obeyed. The boys got up, yawning and rubbing their eyes, having a wholesome dread of their tyrant and his stick, which no tenderness of heart ever made him reluctant to use. Their toilet did not require long to make. The padrone was quite indifferent whether they were clean or not, and offered them no facilities for washing.

When they were dressed they were supplied with a frugal breakfast—a piece of bread and cheese each; their instruments were given them, and they were started off for a long day of toil.

Phil looked around for Giacomo, who had slept in a different room, but he was not to be seen.

"Is Giacomo sick this morning, Pietro?" he asked of the padrone's nephew.

"He pretends to be sick, little drone!" said Pietro, unfeelingly. "If I were the padrone, I would let him taste the stick again."

Phil felt that he would like to see the brutal speaker suffering the punishment he wanted inflicted on him; but he knew Pietro's power and malice too well to give utterance to the wish. A longing came to him to see Giacomo before he went out. He might have had a secret presentiment of what was coming.

"Signor Pietro," he said, "may I see Giacomo before I go out?"

This request would have been refused without doubt, but that Pietro felt flattered at being addressed as signor, to which his years did not yet entitle him. Phil knew this, and therefore used the title.

"What do you want to see him for?" he asked, suspiciously.

"I want to ask him how he feels."

"Yes, you can go in. Tell him he must get up to-morrow. The padrone will not let him spend his time in idleness."

So Phil, having already his fiddle under his arm, entered the room where Giacomo lay. The other occupants of the room had risen, and the little boy was lying on a hard pallet in the corner. His eyes lighted up with joy as he saw Phil enter.

"I am glad it is you, Filippo," he said; "I thought it was the padrone, come to make me get up."

"How do you feel this morning, Giacomo?"

"I do not feel well, Filippo. My back is sore, and I am so weak."

His eyes were very bright with the fever that had now control, and his cheeks were hot and flushed. Phil put his hand upon them.

"Your cheeks are very hot, Giacomo," he said. "You are going to be sick."

"I know it, Filippo," said the little boy. "I may be very sick."

"I hope not, Giacomo."

"Lean over, Filippo," said Giacomo. "I want to tell you something."

Phil leaned over until his ear was close to the mouth of his little comrade.

"I think I am going to die, Filippo," whispered Giacomo.

Phil started in dismay.

"No, no, Giacomo," he said; "that is nonsense. You will live a great many years."

"I think you will, Filippo. You are strong. But I have always been weak, and lately I am tired all the time. I don't care to live—very much. It is hard to live;" and the little boy sighed as he spoke.

"You are too young to die, Giacomo. It is only because you are sick that you think of it. You will soon be better."

"I do not think so, Filippo. I should like to live for one thing."

"What is that?" asked Phil, gazing with strange wonder at the patient, sad face of the little sufferer, who seemed so ready to part with the life which, in spite of his privations and hardships, seemed so bright to him.

"I should like to go back to my home in Italy, and see my mother again before I die. She loved me."

The almost unconscious emphasis which he laid on the word "she" showed that in his own mind he was comparing her with his father, who had sold him into such cruel slavery.

"If you live, Giacomo, you will go back and see her some day."

"I shall never see her again, Filippo," said the little boy, sadly. "If you ever go back to Italy—when you are older—will you go and see her, and tell her that—that I thought of her when I was sick, and wanted to see her?"

"Yes, Giacomo," said Phil, affected by his little companion's manner.

"Filippo!" called Pietro, in harsh tones.

"I must go," said Phil, starting to his feet.

"Kiss me before you go," said Giacomo.

Phil bent over and kissed the feverish lips of the little boy, and then hurried out of the room. He never saw Giacomo again; and this, though he knew it not, was his last farewell to his little comrade.

So Phil commenced his wanderings. He was free in one way— he could go where he pleased. The padrone did not care where he picked up his money, as long as he brought home a satisfactory amount. Phil turned to go up town, though he had no definite destination in view. He missed Giacomo, who lately had wandered about in his company, and felt lonely without him.

"Poor Giacomo!" he thought. "I hope he will be well soon."

"Avast there, boy!" someone called. "Just come to anchor, and give us a tune."

Phil looked up and saw two sailors bearing down upon him (to use a nautical phrase) with arms locked, and evidently with more liquor aboard than they could carry steadily.

"Give us a tune, boy, and we'll pay you," said the second.

Phil had met such customers before, and knew what would please them. He began playing some lively dancing tunes, with so much effect that the sailors essayed to dance on the sidewalk, much to the amusement of a group of boys who collected around them.

"Go it, bluejacket! Go it, boots!" exclaimed the boys, designating them by certain prominent articles of dress.

The applause appeared to stimulate them to further efforts, and they danced and jumped high in air, to the hilarious delight of their juvenile spectators. After a time such a crowd collected that the attention of a passing policeman was attracted.

"What's all this disturbance?" he demanded, in tones of authority.

"We're stretching our legs a little, shipmate," said the first sailor.

"Then you'd better stretch them somewhere else than in the street."

"I thought this was a free country," hiccoughed the second.

"You'll find it isn't if I get hold of you," said the officer.

"Want to fight?" demanded the second sailor, belligerently.

"Boy, stop playing," said the policeman. "I don't want to arrest these men unless I am obliged to do it."

Phil stopped playing, and this put a stop to the dance. Finding there was no more to be seen, the crowd also dispersed. With arms again interlocked, the sailors were about to resume their walk, forgetting to "pay the piper." But Phil was not at all bashful about presenting his claims. He took off his cap, and going up to the jolly pair said, "I want some pennies."

Sailors are free with their money. Parsimony is not one of their vices. Both thrust their hands into their pockets, and each drew out a handful of scrip, which they put into Phil's hands, without looking to see how much it might be.

"That's all right, boy, isn't it?" inquired the first.

"All right," answered Phil, wondering at their munificence. He only anticipated a few pennies, and here looked to be as much as he was generally able to secure in a day. As soon as he got a good chance he counted it over, and found four half dollars, three quarters, and four tens—in all, three dollars and fifteen cents. At this rate, probably, the sailors' money would not last long. However this was none of Phil's business. It was only nine o'clock in the forenoon, and he had already secured enough to purchase immunity from blows at night. Still there was one thing unsatisfactory about it. All this money was to go into the hands of the padrone. Phil himself would reap none of the benefit, unless he bought his dinner, as he had purchased supper the evening before. But for this he had been severely punished, though he could not feel that he had done very wrong in spending the money he himself earned. However, it would be at least three hours before the question of dinner would come up.

He put the money into the pocket of his ragged vest, and walked on.

It was not so cold as the day before. The thermometer had risen twenty-five degrees during the night—a great change, but not unusual in our variable climate. Phil rather enjoyed this walk, notwithstanding his back was a little lame.

He walked up the Bowery to the point where Third and Fourth avenues converge into it. He kept on the left-hand side, and walked up Fourth Avenue, passing the Cooper Institute and the Bible House, and, a little further on, Stewart's magnificent marble store. On the block just above stood a book and periodical store, kept, as the sign indicated, by Richard Burnton. Phil paused a moment to look in at the windows, which were filled with a variety of attractive articles. Suddenly he was conscious of his violin being forcibly snatched from under his arm. He turned quickly, and thought he recognized Tim Rafferty, to whom the reader was introduced in the third chapter of this story.

CHAPTER XIII

PHIL FINDS A CAPITALIST

To account for Phil's unexpected loss, I must explain that Tim Rafferty, whose ordinary place of business was in or near the City Hall Park, had been sent uptown on an errand. He was making his way back leisurely, when, just as he was passing Burnton's bookstore, he saw Phil looking in at the window. He immediately recognized him as the little Italian fiddler who had refused to lend him his fiddle, as described in a previous chapter. In his attempt he was frustrated by Paul Hoffman. His defeat incensed him, and he determined, if he ever met Phil again, to "get even with him," as he expressed it. It struck him that this was a good opportunity to borrow his fiddle without leave.

When Phil discovered his loss, he determined to run after the thief.

"Give me back my fiddle!" he cried.

But this Tim was in no hurry to do. As he had longer legs than Phil, the chances were that he would escape. But some distance ahead he saw one of the blue-coated guardians of the public peace, or, in newsboy parlance, a cop, and saw that Phil could easily prove theft against him, as it would be impossible to pass himself off as a fiddler. He must get rid of the violin in some way, and the sooner the better. He threw it into the middle of the street, just as a heavy cart was coming along. The wheels of the ponderous vehicle passed over the frail instrument, crushing it utterly. Phil ran forward to rescue his instrument, but too late. It was spoiled beyond recovery. Phil picked up the pieces mechanically, and took them back with him, but he soon realized that he might as well cast them away again. Meanwhile Tim, satisfied with the mischief he had done, and feeling revenged for his former mortification, walked up a side street, and escaped interference.

Phil had come to one of those crises in human experience when it is necessary to pause and decide what to do next. The fiddle was not a valuable one—in fact, it was a shabby little instrument—but it was Phil's stock in trade. Moreover, it belonged to the padrone, and however innocent Phil might be as regarded its destruction, his tyrannical master was sure to call him to heavy account for it. He was certain to be severely punished, more so than the evening before, and this was not a pleasant prospect to look forward to. The padrone was sure not to forgive an offense like this.

Thinking over these things, a bold suggestion came into Phil's mind. Why need he go back at all? Why should he not take this occasion for breaking his fetters, and starting out into life on his own account? There was nothing alarming in that prospect. He was not afraid but that he could earn his own living, and fare better than he did at present, when out of his earnings and those of his comrades the padrone was growing rich. Other boys had run away, and though some had been brought back, others had managed to keep out of the cruel clutches of their despotic master.

It did not take Phil long to come to a decision. He felt that he should never have a better chance. He had three dollars in his pocket thanks to the generosity of the sailors—and this would last him some time. It would enable him to get out of the city, which would be absolutely necessary, since, if he remained, the padrone would send Pietro for him and get him back.

There was only one regret he had at leaving the padrone. It would part him from his little comrade, Giacomo. Giacomo, at least, would miss him. He wished the little boy could have gone with him, but this, under present circumstances, was impossible. By staying he would only incur a severe punishment, without being able to help his comrade.

It was still but nine o'clock. He had plenty of time before him, as he would not be missed by the padrone until he failed to make his appearance at night. Having no further occasion to go uptown, he decided to turn and walk down into the business portion of the city. He accordingly made his way leisurely to the City Hall Park, when he suddenly bethought himself of Paul Hoffman, who had served as his friend on a former occasion. Besides Giacomo, Paul was the only friend on whom he could rely in the city. Paul was older and had more experience than he, and could, no doubt, give him good advice as to his future plans.

He crossed the Park and Broadway, and kept along on the west side of the street until he reached the necktie stand kept by Paul. The young street merchant did not at first see him, being occupied with a customer, to whom he finally succeeded in selling two neckties; then looking up, he recognized the young fiddler.

61

"How are you, Phil?" he said, in a friendly manner. "Where have you kept yourself? I have not seen you for a long time."

"I have been fiddling," said Phil.

"But I don't see your violin now. What has become of it?"

"It is broken—destroyed," said Phil.

"How did that happen?"

Phil described the manner in which his violin had been stolen.

"Do you know who stole it?"

"It was that boy who tried to take it once in the Park."

"When I stopped him?"

"Yes."

"I know him. It is Tim Rafferty. He is a mean boy; I will pay him up for it."

"I do not care for it now," said Phil.

"But what will your padrone say when you come home without it?"

"He would beat me, but I will not go home."

"What will you do?"

"I will run away."

"Good for you, Phil! I like your spunk," said Paul, heartily. "I wouldn't go back to the old villain if I were you. Where are you going?"

"Away from New York. If I stay here the padrone would catch me."

"How much did you earn with your fiddle when you had it?"

"Two dollars, if it was a good day."

"That is excellent. I'll tell you what, Phil, if you could stay in the city, I would invite you to come and live with us. You could pay your share of the expense, say three or four dollars a week, and keep the rest of your money to buy clothes, and to save."

"I should like it," said Phil; "but if I stay in the city the padrone would get hold of me."

"Has he any legal right to your services?" asked Paul.

Phil looked puzzled. He did not understand the question.

"I mean did your father sign any paper giving you to him?"

"Yes," said Phil, comprehending now.

"Then I suppose he could take you back. You think you must go away from the city, then, Phil?"

"Yes."

"Where do you think of going?"

"I do not know."

"You might go to Jersey—to Newark, which is quite a large city, only ten miles from here."

"I should like to go there."

"I don't think the padrone would send there to find you. But how are you going to make your living—you have lost your fiddle?"

"I can sing."

"But you would make more money with your fiddle."

"Si, signore."

"Don't talk to me in Italian, Phil; I no understand it."

Phil laughed.

"You can speak English much better than most Italian boys."

"Some cannot speak at all. Some speak french, because we all stayed in Paris sometime before we came to America."

"Parlez-vous Francais?"

"Oui, monsieur, un peu.

"Well, I can't. Those three words are all the French I know. But, I say, Phil, you ought to have a fiddle."

"I should like to have one. I should make more money."

"How much would one cost?"

"I don't know."

"I'll tell you what I will do, Phil," said Paul, after a moment's thought. "I know a pawnbroker's shop on Chatham Street where there is a fiddle for sale. I don't think it will cost very much; not more than five dollars. You must buy it."

"I have not five dollars," said Phil.

"Then I will lend you the money. You shall buy it, and when you have earned money enough you shall come back to New York some day and pay me."

"Thank you," said Phil, gratefully. "I will surely pay you."

"Of course you will, Phil," said Paul, confidently. "I can see by your face that you are honest. I don't believe you would cheat your friend."

"I would not cheat you, Signor Paul."

"I see, Phil, you are bound to make an Italian of me. You may just call me Paul, and don't mind about the signor. Now I'll tell you what I propose. I cannot leave my business for an hour and a half. You can go where you please, but come back at that time, and I will take you home to dinner with me. On the way back I will stop with you at the Chatham Street store and ask the price of the violin; then, if it doesn't cost too much, I will buy it."

"All right," said Phil.

"You must come back at twelve o'clock, Phil."

"I will come."

Phil strolled down to the Battery, feeling a little strange without his violin. He was elated with the thought of his coming freedom, and for the first time since he landed in America the future looked bright to him.

CHAPTER XIV

THE TAMBOURINE GIRL

Arriving at Trinity Church, Phil turned into Wall Street, looking about him in a desultory way, for he was at present out of business. Men and boys were hurrying by in different directions, to and from banks and insurance offices, while here and there a lawyer or lawyer's clerk might be seen looking no less busy and preoccupied. If Phil had had three thousand dollars instead of three, he, too, might have been interested in the price of gold and stocks; but his financial education had been neglected, and he could not have guessed within twenty the day's quotations for either.

As he walked along his attention was suddenly drawn to a pair of Italians, a man and a girl of twelve, the former turning a hand-organ, the latter playing a tambourine. There was nothing unusual in the group; but Phil's heart beat quick for in the girl he thought he recognized a playmate from the same village in which he was born and bred.

Outside Trinity Church is where
Phil meets his old friend Lucia.

"Lucia!" he called, eagerly approaching the pair.

The girl turned quickly, and, seeing the young fiddler, let fall her tambourine in surprise.

"Filippo!" she exclaimed, her eyes lighting up with the joy with which we greet a friend's face in a strange land.

"Why did you drop your tambourine, scelerata?" demanded the man, harshly.

Lucia, a pretty, brown-faced girl, did not lose her joyful look even at this rebuke. She stooped and picked up the tambourine, and began to play mechanically, but continued to speak to Filippo.

"How long are you in the city?" asked Phil, speaking, of course, in his native language.

"Only two weeks," answered Lucia. "I am so glad to see you, Filippo."

"When did you come from Italy?"

"I cannot tell. I think it is somewhere about two months."

"And did you see my mother before you came away?" asked Phil, eagerly.

"Yes, Filippo, I saw her. She told me if I saw you to say that she longed for her dear boy to return; that she thought of him day and night."

"Did she say that, Lucia?"

"Yes, Filippo."

"And is my mother well?" asked Phil, anxiously, for he had a strong love for his mother.

"She is well, Filippo—she is not sick, but she is thin, and she looks sad."

"I will go and see her some day," said Phil. "I wish I could see her now."

"When will you go?"

"I don't know; when I am older."

"But where is your fiddle, Filippo?" asked Lucia. "Do you not play?"

Filippo glanced at the organ-grinder, whom he did not dare to take into his confidence. So he answered, evasively:

"Another boy took it. I shall get another this afternoon."

"Are you with the padrone?"

"Yes."

"Come, Lucia," said the man, roughly, ceasing to play, "we must go on."

Lucia followed her companion obediently, reluctant to leave Phil, with whom she desired to converse longer; but the latter saw that her guardian did not wish the conversation to continue, and so did not follow.

This unexpected meeting with Lucia gave him much to think of. It carried back his thoughts to his humble, but still dear, Italian home, and the mother from whom he had never met with anything but kindness, and a longing to see both made him for the moment almost sad. But he was naturally of a joyous temperament, and hope soon returned.

Phil's friend Lucia is singing while an old man plays the organ.

"I will save money enough to go home," he said to himself. "It will not take very much—not more than fifty dollars. I can get it soon if I do not have to pay money to the padrone."

As may be inferred, Phil did not expect to return home in style. A first-class ticket on a Cunarder was far above his expectations. He would be content to go by steerage all the way, and that could probably be done for the sum he named. So his sadness was but brief, and be soon became hopeful again.

He was aroused from his thoughts of home by a hand laid familiarly on his shoulder. Turning, he saw a bootblack, whose adventures have been chronicled in the volume called "Ragged Dick." They had become acquainted some three months before, Dick having acted as a protector to Phil against some rough boys of his own class.

"Been buyin' stocks?" asked Dick.

"I don't know what they are," said Phil, innocently.

"You're a green one," said Dick. "I shall have to take you into my bankin' house and give you some training in business."

"Have you got a bankin' house?" asked Phil, in surprise.

"In course I have. Don't you see it?" pointing to an imposing-looking structure in front of which they were just passing. "My clerks is all hard to work in there, while I go out to take the air for the benefit of my constitushun."

Phil looked puzzled, not quite understanding Dick's chaffing, and looked rather inquiringly at the blacking box, finding it a little difficult to understand why a banker on so large a scale should be blacking boots in the street.

"Shine your boots, sir?" said Dick to a gentleman just passing.

"Not now; I'm in a hurry."

"Blackin' boots is good exercise," continued Dick, answering the doubt in Phil's face. "I do it for the benefit of my health, thus combinin' profit with salubriousness."

"I can't understand such long words," said Phil. "I don't know much English."

"I would talk to you in Italian," said Dick, "only it makes my head ache. What's come of your fiddle? You haven't sold it, and bought Erie shares, have you?"

"A boy stole it from me, and broke it."

"I'd like to lick him. Who was it?"

"I think his name was Tim Rafferty."

"I know him," said Dick. "I'll give him a lickin' next time I see him."

"Can you?" asked Phil, doubtfully, for his enemy was as large as Dick.

"In course I can. My fists are like sledge-hammers. Jest feel my muscle."

Dick straightened out his arm, and Phil felt of the muscle, which was hard and firm.

"It's as tough as a ten-year-old chicken," said Dick. "It won't be healthy for Tim to come round my way. What made him steal your fiddle? He ain't goin' into the musical line, is he?"

"He was angry because I didn't want to lend it to him."

Just then Tim Rafferty himself turned the corner. There was a lull in his business, and he was wandering along the street eating an apple.

"There he is," said Phil, suddenly espying his enemy.

Dick looked up, and saw with satisfaction that Phil was right. Tim had not yet espied either, nor did he till Dick addressed him.

"Are you round collectin' fiddles this mornin'?" he asked.

Tim looked up, and, seeing that his victim had found an able champion, felt anxious to withdraw. He was about to turn back, but Dick advanced with a determined air.

"Jest stop a minute, Tim Rafferty," said he. "I'm a-goin' to intervoo you for the Herald. That's what they do with all the big rascals nowadays."

"I'm in a hurry," said Tim.

"That's what the pickpocket said when the cop was gently persuadin' him to go to the Tombs, but the cop didn't see it. I want the pleasure of your society a minute or two. I hear you're in the music business."

"No, I'm not," said Tim, shortly.

"What made you borrer this boy's fiddle, then?"

"I don't know anything about it," said Tim, in a fright.

"Some folks forgets easy," returned Dick. "I know a man what went into Tiffany's and took up a watch to look at, and carried it off, forgettin' to pay for it. That's what he told the judge the next day, and the judge sent him to the island for a few months to improve his memory. The air over to the island is very good to improve the memory."

"You ought to know," said Tim, sullenly; "you've been there times enough."

"Have I?" said Dick. "Maybe you saw me there. Was it the ninth time you were there, or the tenth?"

"I never was there," said Tim.

"Maybe it was your twin brother." suggested Dick. "What made you break my friend's fiddle? He wouldn't have minded it so much, only it belonged to his grandfather, a noble count, who made boots for a livin'."

"I don't believe he had a fiddle at all," said Tim.

"That's where your forgetfulness comes in," said Dick "Have you forgot the lickin' I gave you last summer for stealin' my blackin' box?"

69

"You didn't lick me," said Tim.

"Then I'll lick you harder next time," said Dick.

"You ain't able," said Tim, who, glancing over his shoulder, saw the approach of a policeman, and felt secure.

"I will be soon," said Dick, who also observed the approach of the policeman. "I'd do it now, only I've got to buy some gold for a friend of mine. Just let me know when it's perfectly convenient to take a lickin'."

Tim shuffled off, glad to get away unharmed, and Dick turned to Phil.

"I'll give him a lickin' the first time I catch him, when there isn't a cop around," he said.

Phil left his friend at this point, for he saw by the clock on Trinity spire that it was time to go back to join Paul Hoffman, as he had agreed. I may here add that Phil's wrongs were avenged that same evening, his friend, Dick, administered to Tim the promised "lickin'" with such good effect that the latter carried a black eye for a week afterwards.

CHAPTER XV

PHIL'S NEW PLANS

As the clock struck twelve Phil reached the necktie stand of his friend, Paul Hoffman.

"Just in time," said Paul. "Are you hungry?"

"A little."

"That's right. You're going to dine with me; and I want you to bring a good appetite with you."

"What will your mother say?" asked Phil, doubtfully.

"Wait and see. If you don't like what she says you can go off without eating. Where have you been?"

"I went down to Wall Street."

"On business?" inquired Paul, with a smile.

"No," said Phil, seriously. "I saw Lucia."

"Who is she?"

"I forgot. You don't know Lucia. She lived in my home in Italy, and I used to play with her. She told me of my mother."

"That's lucky, Phil. I hope your mother is well."

"She is not sick, but she is thin. She thinks of me," said Phil.

"Of course she does. You will go home and see her some day."

"I hope so."

"Of course you will," said Paul, confidently.

"I saw the boy who stole my fiddle," continued Phil.

"Tim Rafferty?"

"Yes."

"What did he say?"

"I was with a bootblack—the one they call 'Ragged Dick.' Do you know him?"

"Yes; I know Dick. He is a bully fellow, always joking."

"Dick wanted to lick him, but a policeman came, and he went away."

"Does Dick know that he stole your fiddle?"

"Yes."

"Then he will be sure to punish him. It will save me the trouble."

The walk was not long. Soon they were at Paul's door.

"I have brought company to dinner, mother," said Paul, entering first.

"I am glad to see you, Phil," said Mrs. Hoffman. "Why have you not come before?"

"How is that, Phil? Will you stay now?" said Paul.

Mrs. Hoffman looked at Paul inquiringly.

"Phil was afraid he would not be welcome," he exclaimed.

"He is always welcome," said Mrs. Hoffman.

"Where is your fiddle?" asked Jimmy.

"A boy took it," said Phil, "and threw it into the street, and a wagon went over it and broke it."

Jimmy was quite indignant for his friend, when the story had been told.

"It's lucky for Tim Rafferty that he is not here," said Paul, "or he might suffer."

"If I was a big boy I'd lick him," said Jimmy, belligerently.

"I never saw you so warlike before, Jimmy," said Paul.

To Phil this sympathy seemed pleasant. He felt that he was in the midst of friends, and friends were not so plentiful as not to be valued.

"What are you going to have for dinner, mother?" asked Paul.

"I am sorry, Paul, that I have no warm meat. I have some cold roast beef, some hot potatoes, and an apple pudding."

"You needn't apologize, mother. That's good enough for anybody. It's as good as Phil gets at his boarding house, I am sure. He has got rather tired of it, and isn't going to stay."

"Are you going to leave the padrone?" asked Mrs. Hoffman, with interest.

"Si, signora," said Phil.

"Will he let you go?"

"I shall run away," said Phil.

"You see, mother, Phil would be sure of a beating if he went home without his fiddle. Now he doesn't like to be beaten, and the padrone gives harder beatings than you do, mother."

"I presume so," said Mrs. Hoffman, smiling. "I do not think I am very severe."

"No, you spoil the rod and spare the child."

"Is Phil going to stay in the city?"

"No; the padrone would get hold of him if he did. He is going to New Jersey to make his fortune."

"But he will need a fiddle."

"I am going to lend him money enough to buy one. I know a pawnbroker who has one for sale. I think I can get it for three or four dollars. When Phil gets it he is going around giving concerts. How much can you make in a day, Phil?"

"Sometimes I make two dollars," answered Phil.

"That is excellent, especially when you are your own padrone. You will be able to save up money. You will have to buy a pocketbook, Phil."

"Where will you sleep, Phil?" asked Jimmy, interested.

Phil shrugged his shoulders. He had not thought of that question particularly.

"I don't know," he said. "I can sleep anywhere."

"Of course he will stop at the first-class hotels, Jimmy," said Paul, "like all men of distinction. I shouldn't wonder if he married an heiress in six months, and went back to Italy on a bridal tour."

"He is too young to be married," said Jimmy, who, it will be perceived, understood everything literally.

"I don't know but he is," said Paul, "but he isn't too old to be hungry. So, mother, whenever dinner is ready we shall be."

"It is all ready except peeling the potatoes, Paul."

"We can do that ourselves. It is good exercise, and will sharpen our appetites. You will have to eat fast or there won't be much left. Jimmy is the most tremendous eater I ever saw, and won't leave much for the rest of us, if we give him the chance."

"Now, Paul," expostulated Jimmy, feeling aggrieved at this charge, "you know I don't eat as much as you do."

"Hear him talk, Phil. I don't eat more than enough to keep a fly alive."

"It must be a pretty large fly, Paul," said Jimmy, slyly.

"Good joke, Jimmy. Mother, you must give Jimmy twelve potatoes to-day instead of the ten he usually eats."

"Oh, Paul, how can you tell such stories?" exclaimed Jimmy, shocked at such an extravagant assertion. Phil laughed, for there was something ludicrous in the idea of Jimmy, who was a slight boy of seven, making away with such a large quantity, and the little boy began to see that it was a joke at his expense.

The dinner went off well. All had a good appetite, and did full justice to Mrs. Hoffman's cookery. The pudding in particular was pronounced a success. It was so flaky and well-seasoned, and the sauce, flavored with lemon, was so good, that everyone except Mrs. Hoffman took a second piece. For the first time since he had left Italy, Phil felt the uncomfortable sensation of having eaten too much. However, with the discomfort was the pleasant recollection of a good dinner, and to the mind of the little fiddler the future brightened, as it is very apt to do under such circumstances, and he felt ready to go out and achieve his fortune.

"Why won't you stop with us to-night, Phil, and start on your journey to-morrow?" asked Mrs. Hoffman. "I am sure Jimmy would be glad of your company."

"Yes, Phil, stay," said Paul.

Phil hesitated. It was a tempting invitation, but, on the other hand, if he remained in the city till the next day he might be in danger from the padrone.

He expressed this fear.

"I am afraid the padrone would catch me," he said.

"No, he won't. You can go out with me and buy the fiddle now, and then come back and play to mother and Jimmy. To-morrow morning I will go with you to the Jersey City Ferry myself, and if we meet the padrone, I'll give him a hint to be off."

Phil still hesitated, but finally yielded to the united request. But it was now one o'clock, and Paul must be back to his business. Phil took his cap and went with him to purchase the fiddle, promising to come back directly.

They went into Chatham Street, and soon halted before a small shop, in front of which were three gilt balls, indicating that it was a pawnbroker's shop.

Entering, they found themselves in a small apartment, about twelve feet front by twenty in depth, completely filled with pawnable articles in great variety a large part, however, consisting of clothing; for when the poor have occasion to raise money at a pawnbroker's, they generally find little in their possession to pawn except their clothing. Here was a shawls pawned for a few shillings by a poor woman whose intemperate husband threw the burden of supporting two young children upon her. Next to it was a black coat belonging to a clerk, who had been out of employment for three months, and now was out of money also. Here was a child's dress, pawned by the mother in dire necessity to save the child from starving. There was a plain gold ring, snatched by a drunken husband from the finger of his poor wife, not to buy food, but to gratify his insatiable craving for drink.

Over this scene of confusion presided a little old man with blear eyes and wrinkled face, but with a sharp glance, fully alive to his own interests. He was an Englishman born, but he had been forty years in America. He will be remembered by those who have read "Paul the Peddler." Though nearly as poverty-stricken in appearance as his poorest customers, the old man was rich, if reports were true. His business was a very profitable one, allowing the most exorbitant rates of interest, and, being a miser, he spent almost nothing on himself, so that his hoards had increased to a considerable amount.

He looked up sharply, as Paul and Phil entered, and scanned them closely with his ferret-like eyes.

CHAPTER XVI

THE FASHIONABLE PARTY

Eliakim Henderson, for this was the pawnbroker's name, did not remember Paul, though on one occasion our hero had called upon him. Nearly all his customers came to pawn articles, not to purchase, and Eliakim naturally supposed that the two boys had come on this errand. Before entering, Paul said to Phil, "Don't say anything; leave me to manage."

As they entered, Phil espied a fiddle hanging up behind the counter, and he saw at a glance that it was better than the one he had been accustomed to play upon. But to his surprise, Paul did not refer to it at first.

"What will you give me on this coat?" asked Paul, indicating the one he had on.

He had no intention of selling it, but preferred to come to the fiddle gradually, that the pawnbroker might not think that was his main object, and so charge an extra price.

Eliakim scanned the garment critically. It was nearly new and in excellent condition, and he coveted it.

"I will give you a dollar," said he, naming a price low enough to advance upon.

"That is too little," said Paul, shaking his head.

"I might give you fifty cents more, but I should lose if you didn't redeem it."

"I don't think you would. I paid ten dollars for it."

"But it is old."

"No, it isn't; I have only had it a few weeks."

"How much do you want on it?" asked Eliakim, scanning Paul sharply, to see how much he seemed in want of money.

"I don't want any to-day. If I should want some next week, I will come in."

"It will be older next week," said Eliakim, not wanting to lose the bargain, for he hoped it would not be redeemed.

"Never mind; I can get along till then."

"Can I do no business with you this morning?" asked Eliakim, disappointed.

"I don't know," said Paul, looking carelessly around. "My friend here would like a fiddle, if he can get one cheap. What do you ask for that one up there?"

Eliakim took down the fiddle with alacrity. He had had it on hand for a year without securing a customer. It had originally been pawned by a poor musician, for a dollar and a quarter, but the unfortunate owner had never been able to redeem it. Among his customers, the pawnbroker had not found one sufficiently musical to take it off his hands. Here was a slight chance, and he determined to effect a sale if he could.

"It is a splendid instrument," he said, enthusiastically, brushing off the dust with a dirty cotton handkerchief. "I have had many chances to sell it."

"Why didn't you sell it, then?" demanded Paul, who did not believe a word of this.

"Because it was only pawned. I kept it for the owner."

"Oh, well; if you can't sell it, it doesn't matter."

"It is for sale now," said Eliakim, quickly. "He has not come for it, and I shall keep it no longer. Just try it. See what a sp-l-endid instrument it is!" said the pawnbroker, dwelling on the adjective to give emphasis to it.

Paul tried it, but not knowing how to play, of course created only discord. He did not offer it to Phil, because the young Italian boy would have made it sound too well and so enhanced the price.

"It don't sound very well," said he, indifferently; "but I suppose it will do to learn on. What do you want for it?"

"Five dollars," said Eliakim, studying the face of Paul, to observe the effect of his announcement.

"Five dollars," repeated Paul. "Take it back, then, and wait till A. T. Stewart wants one. I haven't got five dollars to throw away."

But the pawnbroker did not expect to get his first price. He named it, in order to have a chance to fall.

"Stay," he said, as Paul made a motion to leave; "what will you give me for it?"

"I'll give you a dollar and a half," said Paul, turning back.

"A dollar and a half!" exclaimed Eliakim, holding up both hands in horror. "Do you want to ruin me?"

"No, I think you want to ruin me. I am willing to pay a fair price."

"You may have it for three dollars and a half."

"No doubt you'd be glad to get that. Come, Phil, we'll go."

"Stay; you may have it for three dollars, though I shall lose by it."

"So should I, if I paid you that price. I can wait till some other time."

But Eliakim did not intend to let this chance slip. He had found the fiddle rather unsalable, and feared if he lost his chance of disposing of it, it might remain on his hands for a year more. He was willing, therefore, to take less than the profit he usually calculated upon in the sale of articles which remained unredeemed.

"You may have it for two dollars and a half," he said.

As far as Paul could judge, though he did not know much about the price of violins, this was a reasonable price. But he knew that Eliakim must have got it for considerably less, or he would not so soon have come down to this sum. He did not hesitate, therefore, to try to get it a little cheaper.

"I'll give you two dollars and a quarter," he said, "and not a penny more."

Eliakim tried hard to get ten cents more, but Paul saw that he was sure of his purchase, and remained obdurate. So, after a pretense of putting up the fiddle, the pawnbroker finally said, "You may have it, but I tell you that I shall lose money."

"All right," said Paul; "hand it over."

"Where is the money?" asked Eliakim, cautiously.

Paul drew from his pocket a two-dollar bill and twenty-five cents in currency, and received the fiddle. The pawnbroker scrutinized the money closely, fearing that it might be bad; but finally, making up his mind on that point, deposited it in his money drawer.

"Well, Phil, we may as well go," said Paul. "We've got through our business."

The pawnbroker heard this, and a sudden suspicion entered his mind that Paul had been too sharp for him.

"I might have got twenty-five cents more," he thought regretfully; and this thought disturbed the complacency he felt at first.

"Well, Phil, how do you like it?" asked Paul, as they emerged into the street.

"Let me try it," said Phil, eagerly.

He struck up a tune, which he played through, his face expressing the satisfaction he felt.

"Is it as good as your old one?"

"It is much better," said Phil. "I will pay you for it;" and he drew out the money the sailors had given him in the morning.

"No, Phil," said his friend, "you may need that money. Keep it, and pay me when you have more."

"But I shall be away."

"You will come to the city some day. When you do you will know where to find me. Now go and play a tune to Jimmy. He is waiting for you. If you remain in the streets, your old enemy, Tim Rafferty, may want to borrow your fiddle again."

"You are very kind to me, Paolo," said Phil, raising his dark eyes with a sudden impulse of gratitude.

"It's nothing, Phil," said Paul, modestly; "you would do the same for me if I needed it."

"Yes, I would," said Phil; "but I am poor, and I cannot help you."

"You won't be poor always, Phil," said Paul, cheerfully, "nor I either, I hope. I mean to be a merchant some time on a bigger scale than now. As for you, you will be a great player, and give concerts at the Academy of Music."

Phil laughed, but still seemed pleased at the prophecy.

"Well, Phil, I must bid you good-by for a little while, or my clerks will be cheating me. I will see you at supper."

"Addio, Paolo," said Phil.

"Addio," said Paul, laughing. "Wouldn't I make a good Italian?"

Paul returned to his stand, and Phil took the direction of Mrs. Hoffman's rooms. While on his way he heard the sound of a hand-organ, and, looking across the way, saw, with some uneasiness, his old enemy Pietro, playing to a crowd of boys.

"I hope he won't see me," said Phil to himself.

He was afraid Pietro would remember his old violin, and, seeing the difference in the instrument he now had, inquire how he got it. He might, if not satisfied on this point, take Phil home with him, which would be fatal to his plans. He thought it prudent, therefore, to turn down the next street, and get out of sight as soon as possible. Fortunately for him Pietro had his back turned, so that he did not observe him. Nothing would have pleased him better than to get the little fiddler into trouble, for, besides being naturally malicious, he

—

79

felt that an exhibition of zeal in his master's service would entitle him to additional favors at the hands of the padrone, whom he hoped some day to succeed.

"Oh, what a beautiful fiddle!" said Jimmy, in admiration, as Phil reappeared. "Do you think I could play on it?"

Phil shook his head, smiling.

"Don't let Jimmy have it. He would only spoil it," said Mrs. Hoffman. "I don't think he would succeed as well in music as in drawing."

"Will you play something?" asked Jimmy.

Phil willingly complied, and for half an hour held Jimmy entranced with his playing. The little boy then undertook to teach Phil how to draw, but at this Phil probably cut as poor a figure as his instructor would have done at playing on the violin.

So the afternoon wore away, happily for all three, and at five Paul made his appearance. When supper was over Phil played again, and this attracting the attention of the neighbors, Mrs. Hoffman's rooms were gradually filled with visitors, who finally requested Phil to play some dancing tunes. Finding him able to do so, an impromptu dance was got up, and Mrs. Hoffman, considerably to her surprise, found that she was giving a dancing-party. Paul, that nothing might be left out, took a companion with him and they soon reappeared with cake and ice cream, which were passed around amid great hilarity; and it was not until midnight that the last visitor went out, and the sound of music and laughter was hushed.

"You are getting fashionable in your old age, mother," said Paul, gayly. "I think I shall send an account of your party to the Home Journal."

"I believe it is usual to describe the dresses of the ladies," said Mrs. Hoffman, smiling.

"Oh, yes, I won't forget that. Just give me a piece of paper and see how I will do it."

Paul, whose education, I repeat here, was considerably above that of most boys in his position, sat down and hastily wrote the following description, which was read to the great amusement of his auditors:

"Mrs. Hoffman, mother of the well-known artist, Jimmy Hoffman, Esq., gave a fashionable party last evening. Her spacious and elegant apartments were crowded with finely dressed gentlemen and ladies from the lower part of the city. Signor Filippo, the great

Italian musician, furnished the music. Mrs. Hoffman appeared in a costly calico dress, and had a valuable gold ring on one of her fingers. Her son, the artist, was richly dressed in a gray suit, purchased a year since. Miss Bridget Flaherty, of Mott Street, was the belle of the occasion, and danced with such grace and energy that the floor came near giving away beneath her fairy tread. [Miss Flaherty, by the way, weighed one hundred and eighty pounds.] Mr. Mike Donovan, newspaper merchant, handed round refreshments with his usual graceful and elegant deportment. Miss Matilda Wiggins appeared in a magnificent print dress, imported from Paris by A. T. Stewart, and costing a shilling a yard. No gloves were worn, as they are now dispensed with in the best society. At a late hour the guests dispersed. Mrs. Hoffman's party will long be remembered as the most brilliant of the season."

"I did not know you had so much talent for reporting, Paul," said his mother. "You forgot one thing, however."

"What is that?"

"You said nothing of yourself."

"I was too modest, mother. However, if you insist upon it, I will do so. Anything at all to please you."

Paul resumed his writing and in a short time had the following:

"Among those present we observed the handsome and accomplished Paul Hoffman, Esq., the oldest son of the hostess. He was elegantly dressed in a pepper-and-salt coat and vest, blue necktie, and brown breeches, and wore a six-cent diamond breastpin in the bosom of his shirt. His fifteen-cent handkerchief was perfumed with cologne which he imported himself at a cost of ten cents per bottle. He attracted general admiration."

"You seem to have got over your modesty, Paul," said his mother

"I am sleepy," said Jimmy, drowsily rubbing his eyes.

As this expressed the general feeling, they retired to bed at once, and in half an hour were wandering in the land of dreams.

CHAPTER XVII

THE PADRONE IS ANXIOUS

The next morning Paul and Phil rose later that usual. They slept longer, in order to make up for the late hour at which they retired. As they sat down to breakfast, at half-past eight, Paul said: "I wonder whether the padrone misses you, Phil?"

"Yes," said Phil; "he will be very angry because I did not come back last night."

"Will he think you have run away?"

"I do not know. Some of the boys stay away sometimes, because they are too far off to come home."

"Then he may expect you to-night. I suppose he will have a beating ready for you."

"Yes, he would beat me very hard," said Phil, "if he thought I did not mean to come back."

"I should like to go and tell him that he need not expect you. I should like to see how he looks."

"He might beat you, too, Paolo."

"I should like to see him try it," said Paul, straightening up with a consciousness of strength. "He might find that rather hard."

Phil looked admiringly at the boy who was not afraid of the padrone. Like his comrades, he had been accustomed to think of the padrone as possessed of unlimited power, and never dreamed of anybody defying him, or resisting his threats. Though he had determined to run away, his soul was not free from the tyranny of his late taskmaster, and he thought with uneasiness and dread of the possibility of his being conveyed back to him.

Well, mother," said Paul, glancing at the clock as he rose from the breakfast table, "it is almost nine o'clock—rather a late hour for a business man like me."

"You are not often so late, Paul."

"It is lucky that I am my own employer, or I might run the risk of being discharged. I am afraid the excuse that I was at Mrs. Hoffman's fashionable party would not be thought sufficient. I guess I won't have time to stop to shave this morning."

"You haven't got anything to shave," said Jimmy.

"Don't be envious, Jimmy. I counted several hairs this morning. Well, Phil, are you ready to go with me? Don't forget your fiddle."

"When shall we see you again, Philip?" said Mrs. Hoffman.

"I do not know," said the little minstrel.

"Shall you not come to the city sometimes?"

"I am afraid the padrone would catch me," said Phil.

"Whenever you do come, Phil," said Paul, "come right to me. I will take care of you. I don't think the padrone will carry us both off, and he would have to take me if he took you."

"Good-by, Philip," said Mrs. Hoffman, offering her hand. "I hope you will prosper."

"So do I, Phil," said Jimmy.

Phil thus took with him the farewells and good wishes of two friends who had been drawn to him by his attractive face and good qualities. He could not help wishing that he might stay with them permanently, but he knew that this could not be. To remain in the same city with the padrone was out of the question.

Meanwhile we return to the house, which Phil had forsaken, and inquire what effect was produced by his non-appearance.

It was the rule of the establishment that all the boys should be back by midnight. Phil had generally returned an hour before that time. When, therefore, it was near midnight, the padrone looked uneasily at the clock.

"Have you seen Filippo?" he asked, addressing his nephew.

"No, signore," answered Pietro. "Filippo has not come in."

"Do you think he has run away?" asked the padrone, suspiciously.

"I don't know," said Pietro.

"Have you any reason to think he intended to run away?"

"No," said Pietro.

"I should not like to lose him. He brings me more money than most of the boys."

"He may come in yet."

"When he does," said the padrone, frowning, "I will beat him for being so late. Is there any boy that he would be likely to tell, if he meant to run away?"

"Yes," said Pietro, with a sudden thought, "there is Giacomo."

"The sick boy?"

"Yes. Filippo went in this morning to speak to him. He might have told him then."

"That is true. I will go and ask him."

Giacomo still lay upon his hard pallet, receiving very little attention. His fever had increased, and he was quite sick. He rolled from one side to the other in his restlessness. He needed medical attention, but the padrone was indifferent, and none of the boys would have dared to call a doctor without his permission. As he lay upon his bed, the padrone entered the room with a hurried step.

"Where is Giacomo?" he demanded, harshly.

"Here I am, signore padrone," answered the little boy, trembling, as he always did when addressed by the tyrant.

"Did Filippo come and speak with you this morning, before he went out?"

"Si, signore."

"What did he say?"

"He asked me how I felt."

"What did you tell him?"

"I told him I felt sick."

"Nothing more?"

"I told him I thought I should die.'

"Nonsense!" said the padrone, harshly; "you are a coward. You have a little cold, that is all. Did he say anything about running away?"

"No, signore."

"Don't tell me a lie!" said the tyrant, frowning.

"I tell you the truth, signore padrone. Has not Filippo come home?"

"No."

I do not think he has run away," said the little boy.

"Why not?"

"I think he would tell me."

"So you two are friends, are you?"

"Si, signore; I love Filippo," answered Giacomo, speaking the last words tenderly, and rather to himself than to the padrone. He looked up to Phil, though little older than himself, with a mixture of respect and devotion, leaning upon him as the weak are prone to lean upon the strong.

"Then you will be glad to hear," said the padrone, with a refinement of cruelty, "that I shall beat him worse than last night for staying out so late."

"Don't beat him, padrone," pleaded Giacomo, bursting into tears. "Perhaps he cannot come home."

"Did he ever speak to you of running away?" asked the padrone, with a sudden thought.

Giacomo hesitated. He could not truthfully deny that Filippo had done so, but he did not want to get his friend into trouble. He remained silent, looking up at the tyrant with troubled eyes.

"Why do you not speak? Did you hear my question?" asked the padrone, with a threatening gesture.

Had the question been asked of some of the other boys present, they would not have scrupled to answer falsely; but Giacomo had a religious nature, and, neglected as he had been, he could not make up his mind to tell a falsehood. So, after a pause, he faltered out a confession that Phil had spoken of flight.

"Do you hear that, Pietro?" said the padrone, turning to his nephew. "The little wretch has doubtless run away."

"Shall I look for him to-morrow?" asked Pietro, with alacrity, for to him it would be a congenial task to drag Phil home, and witness the punishment.

"Yes, Pietro. I will tell you where to go in the morning. We must have him back, and I will beat him so that he will not dare to run away again."

The padrone would have been still more incensed could he have looked into Mrs. Hoffman's room and seen the little fiddler the center of a merry group, his brown face radiant with smiles as he swept the chords of his violin. It was well for Phil that he could not see him.

CHAPTER XVIII

PHIL ELUDES HIS PURSUER

Phil had already made up his mind where to go. Just across the river was New Jersey, with its flourishing towns and cities, settled to a large extent by men doing business in New York. The largest of these cities was Newark, only ten miles distant. There Phil decided to make his first stop. If he found himself in danger of capture he could easily go farther. This plan Paul approved, and it was to be carried into execution immediately.

**Phil and Paul see Pietro standing on the docks
when they leave on the Cortlandt Street Ferry.**

"I will go down to the Cortlandt Street Ferry with you, Phil," said Paul.

"I should like to have you, if it will not take you from your business, Paolo."

"My business can wait," said Paul. "I mean to see you safe out of the city. The padrone may be in search of you already."

"I think he will send Pietro to find me," said Phil.

"Who is Pietro?"

Phil explained that Pietro was the padrone's nephew and assisted in oppressing the boys.

"I hope he will send him," said Paul.

Phil looked up in surprise.

"I should like to see this Pietro. What would he do if he should find you?"

"He would take me back."

"If you did not want to go?"

"I couldn't help it," said Phil, shrugging his shoulders. "He is much bigger than I."

"Is he bigger than I am?"

"I think he is as big."

"He isn't big enough to take you away if I am with you."

Paul did not say this boastfully, but with a quiet confidence in his own powers in which he was justified. Though by no means quarrelsome, he had on several occasions been forced in self-defense into a contest with boys of his own size, and in some instances larger, and in every case he had acquitted himself manfully, and come off victorious.

"I should not be afraid if you were with me, Paolo," said Phil.

"You are right, Phil," said Paul, approvingly. "But here we are at the ferry."

Cortlandt Street is a short distance below the Astor House, and leads to the ferry, connecting on the other side with trains bound for Philadelphia and intermediate places.

Paul paid the regular toll, and passed through the portal with Phil.

"Are you going with me?" asked the little fiddler, in surprise.

"Only to Jersey City, Phil. There might be some of your friends on board the boat. I want to see you safe on the cars. Then I must leave you."

"You are very kind, Paolo."

"You are a good little chap, Phil, and I mean to help you. But the boat is about ready to start. Let us go on board."

They walked down the pier, and got on the boat a minute before it started. They did not pass through to the other end, but, leaning against the side, kept their eyes fixed on the city they were about to leave. They had not long to wait. The signal was heard, and the boat started leisurely from the pier. It was but ten feet distant, when the attention of Paul and Phil was drawn to a person running down the drop in great haste. He evidently wanted to catch the boat, but was too late.

Phil clutched at Paul's arm, and pointed to him in evident excitement.

"It is Pietro," he said.

At that moment Pietro, standing on the brink, caught sight of the boy he was pursuing, looking back at him from the deck of the ferry-boat. A look of exultation and disappointment swept over his face as he saw Phil, but realized that he was out of his reach. He had a hand-organ with him, and this had doubtless encumbered him, and prevented his running as fast as he might otherwise.

"So that is Pietro, is it?" said Paul, regarding him attentively in order to fix his face in his memory.

"Yes, Paolo," said Phil, his eyes fixed nervously upon his pursuer, who maintained his place, and was watching him with equal attention.

"You are not frightened, Phil, are you?"

Phil admitted that he was.

"He will come over in the next boat," he said.

"But he will not know where you are."

"He will seek me."

"Will he? Then I think he will be disappointed. The cars will start on the other side before the next boat arrives. I found out about that before we started."

Phil felt relieved by this intelligence, but still he was nervous. Knowing well Pietro's malice, he dreaded the chances of his capturing him.

"He stays there. He does not go away," said Phil.

"It will do him no good, Phil. He is like a cat watching a canary bird beyond his reach. I don't think he will catch you to-day."

"He may go in the cars, too," suggested Phil.

"That is true. On the whole, Phil, when you get to Newark, I advise you to walk into the country. Don't stay in the city. He might find you there."

"I will do what you say, Paolo. It will be better."

They soon reached the Jersey shore. The railroad station was close by. They went thither at once, and Phil bought a ticket for Newark.

**Phil boards a Pennsylvania Railroad train bound for
Newark while Pietro looks for him in Jersey City.**

"How soon will the cars start?" inquired Paul of a railway official.

"In five minutes," was the answer.

"Then, Phil, I advise you to get into the cars at once. Take a seat on the opposite side, though there is no chance of your being seen by Pietro, who will get here too late. Still, it is best to be on the safe side. I will stay near the ferry and watch Pietro when he lands. Perhaps I will have a little conversation with him."

"I will go, Paolo."

"Well, good-by, Phil, and good luck," said Paul, cheerfully. "If you ever come to New York, come to see me."

"Yes, Paolo, I will be sure to come."

"And, Phil, though I don't think you will ever fall into the power of that old brute again (I am sure you won't if you take good care of yourself), still, if he does get you back again, come to me the first chance you get, and I will see what I can do for you."

"Thank you, Paolo. I will remember your kindness always," said the little fiddler, gratefully.

"That is all right, Phil. Good-by!"

"Good-by!" said Phil, and, shaking the hand of his new friend, he ascended the steps, and took a seat on the opposite side, as Paul had recommended.

"I am sorry to part with Phil," said Paul to himself. "He's a fine little chap, and I like him. If ever that old brute gets hold of him again, he shan't keep him long. Now, Signor Pietro, I'll go back and see you on your arrival."

Phil was right in supposing that Pietro would take passage on the next boat. He waited impatiently on the drop till it touched, and sprang on board. He cursed the interval of delay, fearing that it would give Phil a chance to get away. However, there was no help for this. Time and tide wait for no man, but it often happens that we are compelled to wait for them. But at length the boat touched the Jersey shore, and Pietro sprang out and hurried to the gates, looking eagerly on all sides for a possible glimpse of the boy he sought. He did not see him, for the cars were already on their way, but his eyes lighted up with satisfaction as they lighted on Paul, whom he recognized as the companion of Phil. He had seen him talking to the little fiddler. Probably he would know where he had gone. He walked up to Paul, who was standing near, and, touching his cap, said: "Excuse me, signore, but have you seen my little brother?"

"Your little brother?" repeated Paul, deliberately.

"Si, signore, a little boy with a fiddle. He was so high;" and Pietro indicated the height of Phil correctly by his hand.

"There was a boy came over in the boat with me," said Paul.

"Yes, yes; he is the one, signore," said Pietro, eagerly.

"And he is your brother?"

"Si, signore."

"That's a lie," thought Paul, "I should know it even if Phil had not told me. Phil is a handsome little chap. He wouldn't have such a villainous-looking brother as you."

"Can you tell me where he has gone?" asked Pietro, eagerly.

"Didn't he tell you where he was going?" asked Paul, in turn.

"I think he means to run away," said Pietro. "Did you see where he went?"

"Why should he want to run away?" asked Paul, who enjoyed tantalizing Pietro, who he saw was chafing with impatience. "Did you not treat him well?"

"He is a little rascal," said Pietro. "He is treated well, but he is a thief."

"And you are his brother," repeated Paul, significantly.

"Did you see where he went?" asked Pietro, getting angry. "I want to take him back to his father."

"How should I know?" returned Paul, coolly. "Do you think I have nothing to do but to look after your brother?"

"Why didn't you tell me that before?" said Pietro, incensed.

"Don't get mad," said Paul, indifferently; "it won't do you any good. Perhaps, if you look round, you will see your brother. I'll tell him you want him if I see him."

Pietro looked at Paul suspiciously. It struck him that the latter might be making a fool of him, but Paul looked so utterly indifferent that he could judge nothing from his appearance. He concluded that Phil was wandering about somewhere in Jersey City.

It did not occur to him that he might have taken the cars for some more distant place. At any rate, there seemed no chance of getting any information out of Paul. So he adjusted his hand-organ and walked up the street leading from the ferry, looking sharply on either side, hoping to catch a glimpse of the runaway; but, of course, in vain.

Phil often earns money while riding back and forth on the Brooklyn Ferry and singing for the passengers.

"I don't think you'll find Phil to-day, Signor Pietro," said Paul to himself, as he watched his receding form. "Now, as there is nothing more to be done here, I will go back to business."

CHAPTER XIX

PIETRO'S PURSUIT

The distance from New York to Newark is but ten miles. Phil had been there once before with an older boy. He was at no loss, therefore, as to the proper place to get out. He stepped from the cars and found himself in a large depot. He went out of a side door, and began to wander about the streets of Newark. Now, for the first time, he felt that he was working for himself, and the feeling was an agreeable one. True, he did not yet feel wholly secure. Pietro might possibly follow in the next train. He inquired at the station when the next train would arrive.

"In an hour," was the reply.

It would be an hour, therefore, before Pietro could reach Newark.

He decided to walk on without stopping till he reached the outskirts of the city, and not venture back till nightfall, when there would be little or no danger.

Accordingly he plodded on for an hour and a half, till he came where the houses were few and scattered at intervals. In a business point of view this was not good policy, but safety was to be consulted first of all. He halted at length before a grocery store, in front of which he saw a small group of men standing. His music was listened to with attention, but when he came to pass his cap round afterward the result was small. In fact, to be precise, the collection amounted to but eight cents.

"How's business, boy?" asked a young man who stood at the door in his shirt-sleeves, and was evidently employed in the grocery.

"That is all I have taken," said Phil, showing the eight cents.

"Did you come from New York this morning?"

"Yes."

"Then you haven't got enough to pay for your ticket yet?"

Phil shrugged his shoulders.

"I don't believe you'll make your fortune out here."

Phil was of precisely the same opinion, but kept silent.

"You would have done better to stay in New York."

To this also Phil mentally assented, but there were imperative reasons, as we know, for leaving the great city.

It was already half-past twelve, and Phil began, after his walk, to feel the cravings of appetite. He accordingly went into the grocery and bought some crackers and cheese, which he sat down by the stove and ate.

The boys warm themselves by the stove in a grocery store, over the objection of the owner.

"Are you going farther?" asked the same young man who had questioned him before.

"I shall go back to Newark to-night," said Phil.

"Let me try your violin."

"Can you play?" asked Phil, doubtfully, for he feared that an unpracticed player might injure the instrument.

"Yes, I can play. I've got a fiddle at home myself."

Our hero surrendered his fiddle to the young man, who played passably.

"You've got a pretty good fiddle," he said. "I think it's better than mine. Can you play any dancing tunes?"

Phil knew one or two, and played them.

"If you were not going back to Newark, I should like to have you play with me this evening. I don't have anybody to practice with."

"I would not know where to sleep," said Phil, hesitatingly.

"Oh, we've got beds enough in our house. Will you stay?"

Phil reflected that he had no place to sleep in Newark except such as he might hire, and decided to accept the offer of his new friend.

"This is my night off from the store," he said. "I haven't got to come back after supper. Just stay around here till six o'clock. Then I'll take you home and give you some supper, and then we'll play this evening."

Phil had no objection to this arrangement. In fact, it promised to be an agreeable one for him. As he was sure of a supper, a bed and breakfast, there was no particular necessity for him to earn anything more that day. However, he went out for an hour or two, and succeeded in collecting twenty-five cents. He realized, however, that it was not so easy to pick up pennies in the country as in the city— partly because population is sparser and partly because, though there is less privation in the country, there is also less money.

A little before six Phil's new friend, whose name he ascertained was Edwin Grover, washed his hands, and, putting on his coat, said "Come along, Phil."

Phil, who had been sitting near the stove, prepared to accompany him.

"We haven't got far to go," said Edwin, who was eighteen. "I am glad of that, for the sooner I get to the supper table the better."

After five minutes' walk they stopped at a comfortable two-story house near the roadside.

"That's where I put up," said Edwin.

He opened the door and entered, followed by Phil, who felt a little bashful, knowing that he was not expected.

"Have you got an extra plate, mother?" asked Edwin. "This is a professor of the violin, who is going to help me make some music this evening."

"He is welcome," said Mrs. Grover, cheerfully, "We can make room for him. He is an Italian, I suppose. What is your name?"

"Filippo."

"I will call you Philip. I suppose that is the English name. Will you lay down your violin and draw up to the fire?"

"I am not cold," said Phil.

"He is not cold, he is hungry, as Ollendorf says," said Edwin, who had written a few French exercises according to Ollendorf's system. "Is supper almost ready?"

"It will be ready at once. There is your father coming in at the front gate, and Henry with him."

Mr. Grover entered, and Phil made the acquaintance of the rest of the family. He soon came to feel that he was a welcome guest, and shared in the family supper, which was well cooked and palatable. Then Edwin brought out his fiddle, and the two played various tunes. Phil caught one or two new dancing tunes from his new friend, and in return taught him an Italian air. Three or four people from a neighboring family came in, and a little impromptu dance was got up. So the evening passed pleasantly, and at half-past ten they went to bed, Phil sleeping in a little room adjoining that in which the brothers Edwin and Harry slept.

After breakfast the next morning Phil left the house, with a cordial invitation to call again when he happened to be passing.

Before proceeding with his adventures, we must go back to Pietro.

He, as we know, failed to elicit any information from Paul likely to guide him in his pursuit of Phil. He was disappointed. Still, he reflected that Phil had but a quarter of an hour's start of him— scarcely that, indeed—and if he stopped to play anywhere, he would doubtless easily find him. There was danger, of course, that he would turn off somewhere, and Pietro judged it best to inquire whether such a boy had passed.

Seeing two boys playing in the street, he inquired: "Have you seen anything of my little brother?"

"What does he look like?" inquired one.

"He is not quite so large as you. He had a fiddle with him."

"No, I haven't seen him. Have you, Dick?"

"Yes," said the other, "there was a boy went along with a fiddle."

This was true, but, as we know, it was not Phil.

"Did you see where he went?" demanded Pietro, eagerly.

"Straight ahead," was the reply.

Lured by the delusive hope these words awakened, Pietro went on. He did not stop to play on his organ. He was too intent on finding Phil. At length, at a little distance before him, he saw a figure about the size of Phil, playing on the violin. He hurried forward elated, but when within a few yards he discovered to his disappointment that it was not Phil, but a little fiddler of about his size. He was in the employ of a different padrone. He was doubtless the one the boy had seen.

The Organ Grinder, No. 1

Overpeck

HAMILTON, O.

Pietro sees Phil, but he's unable to catch him because he has to run while carrying his hand organ, like the one in this picture.

Disappointed, Pietro now turned back, and bent his steps to the ferry. But he saw nothing of Phil on the way.

"I would like to beat him, the little wretch!" he said to himself, angrily. "If I had not been too late for the boat, I would have easily caught him."

It never occurred to Pietro that Phil might have taken the cars for a more distant point, as he actually did. The only thing he could think of, for he was not willing to give up the pursuit, was to go back. He remained in Jersey City all day, wandering about the streets, peering here and there; but he did not find Phil, for a very good reason.

The padrone awaited his report at night with some impatience. Phil was one of the smartest boys he had, and he had no mind to lose him.

"Did you find him, Pietro?" he asked as soon as his nephew entered his presence.

"I saw him," said Pietro.

"Then why did you not bring him back?"

Pietro explained the reason. His uncle listened attentively.

"Pietro, you are a fool," he said, at length.

"Why am I a fool?" asked Pietro, sullenly.

"Because you sought Filippo where he is not."

"Where is he?"

"He did not stop in Jersey City. He went farther. He knew that you were on his track. Did you ask at the station if such a boy bought a ticket?"

"I did not think of it."

"Then you were a fool."

"What do you want me to do?"

"Tomorrow you must go to Newark. That is the first large town. I must have Filippo back."

"I will go," said Pietro, briefly.

He was mortified at the name applied to him by his uncle, as well as by the fact of Phil's having thus far outwitted him. He secretly determined that when he did get him into his power he would revenge himself for all the trouble to which he had been put, and there was little doubt that he would keep his word.

CHAPTER XX

PIETRO'S DISAPPOINTMENT

Though Phil had not taken in much money during the first day of independence, he had more than paid his expenses. He started on the second day with a good breakfast, and good spirits. He determined to walk back to Newark, where he might expect to collect more money than in the suburbs. If he should meet Pietro he determined not to yield without a struggle. But he felt better now than at first, and less afraid of the padrone.

Nine o'clock found him again in Newark. He soon came to a halt, and began to play. A few paused to listen, but their interest in music did not extend so far as to affect their pockets. Phil passed around his hat in vain. He found himself likely to go unrewarded for his labors. But just then he noticed a carriage with open door, waiting in front of a fashionable dry-goods store. Two ladies had just come out and taken their seats preparatory to driving off, when Phil stepped up bareheaded and held his cap. He was an unusually attractive boy, and as he smiled one of the ladies, who was particularly fond of children, noticed him.

"What a handsome boy!" she said to her companion.

"Some pennies for music," said Phil.

"How old are you?" asked the lady.

"Twelve years."

"Just the age of my Johnny. If I give you some money what will you do with it?"

"I will buy dinner," said Phil.

"I never give to vagrants," said the second lady, a spinster of uncertain age, who did not share her niece's partiality for children.

"It isn't his fault if he is a vagrant, Aunt Maria," said the younger lady.

"I have no doubt he is a thief," continued Aunt Maria, with acerbity.

"I am not a thief," said Phil, indignantly, for he understood very well the imputation, and he replaced his cap on his head.

"I don't believe you are," said the first lady; "here, take this," and she put in his hand twenty-five cents.

"Thank you, signora," said Phil, with a grateful smile.

"That money is thrown away," said the elderly lady; "you are very indiscriminate in your charity, Eleanor."

"It is better to give too much than too little, Aunt Maria, isn't it?"

"You shouldn't give to unworthy objects."

"How do you know this boy is an unworthy object?"

"He is a young vagrant."

"Can he help it? It is the way he makes his living."

The discussion continued, but Phil did not stop to hear it. He had received more than he expected, and now felt ready to continue his business. One thing was fortunate, and relieved him from the anxiety which he had formerly labored under. He was not obliged to obtain a certain sum in order to escape a beating at night. He had no master to account to. He was his own employer, as long as he kept out of the clutches of the padrone.

Phil continued to roam about the streets very much after the old fashion, playing here and there as he thought it expedient. By noon he had picked up seventy-five cents, and felt very well satisfied with his success. But if, as we are told, the hour that is darkest is just before day, it also happens sometimes that danger lies in wait for prosperity, and danger menaced our young hero, though he did not know it. To explain this, we must go back a little.

When Pietro prepared to leave the lodging-house in the morning, the padrone called loudly to him.

"Pietro," said he, "you must find Filippo today."

"Where shall I go?" asked Pietro.

"Go to Newark. Filippo went there, no doubt, while you, stupid that you are, went looking for him in Jersey City. You have been in Newark before?"

"Yes, signore padrone."

"Very good; then you need no directions."

"If I do not find him in Newark, where shall I go?"

"He is in Newark," said the padrone, confidently. "He will not leave it."

He judged that Phil would consider himself safe there, and would prefer to remain in a city rather than go into the country.

"I will do my best," said Pietro.

"I expect you to bring him back to-night."

—

99

"I should like to do so," said Pietro, and he spoke the truth. Apart from his natural tendency to play the tyrant over smaller boys, he felt a personal grudge against Phil for eluding him the day before, and so subjecting him to the trouble of another day's pursuit, besides the mortification of incurring a reprimand from his uncle. Never did agent accept a commission more readily than Pietro accepted that of catching and bringing Filippo to the padrone.

Leaving the lodging-house he walked down to the ferry at the foot of Cortlandt Street, and took the first train for Newark. It was ten o'clock before he reached the city. He had nothing in particular to guide him, but made up his mind to wander about all day, inquiring from time to time if anyone had seen his little brother, describing Phil. After a while his inquiries were answered in the affirmative, and he gradually got on the track of our hero.

At twelve o'clock Phil went into a restaurant, and invested thirty cents in a dinner. As the prices were low, he obtained for this sum all he desired. Ten minutes afterward, as he was walking leisurely along with that feeling of tranquil enjoyment which a full stomach is apt to give, Pietro turned the corner behind him. No sooner did the organ-grinder catch sight of his prey, than a fierce joy lighted up his eyes, and he quickened his pace.

"Ah, scelerato, I have you now," he exclaimed to himself. "To-night you shall feel the stick."

But opportunely for himself Phil looked behind him. When he saw Pietro at but a few rods' distance his heart stood still with sudden fright, and for an instant his feet were rooted to the ground. Then the thought of escape came to him, and he began to run, not too soon.

"Stop!" called out Pietro. "Stop, or I will kill you!"

But Phil did not comprehend the advantage of surrendering himself to Pietro. He understood too well how he would be treated, if he returned a prisoner. Instead of obeying the call, he only sped on the faster. Now between the pursuer and the pursued there was a difference of six years, Pietro being eighteen, while Phil was but twelve. This, of course, was in Pietro's favor. On the other hand, the pursuer was encumbered by a hand-organ, which retarded his progress, while Phil had only a violin, which did not delay him at all. This made their speed about equal, and gave Phil a chance to escape, unless he should meet with some interruption.

"Stop!" called Pietro, furiously, beginning to realize that the victory was not yet won.

Phil looked over his shoulder, and, seeing that Pietro was no nearer, took fresh courage. He darted round a corner, with his pursuer half a dozen rods behind him. They were not in the most frequented parts of the city, but in a quarter occupied by two-story wooden houses. Seeing a front door open, Phil, with a sudden impulse, ran hastily in, closing the door behind him.

A woman with her sleeves rolled up, who appeared to have taken her arms from the tub, hearing his step, came out from the back room.

"What do ye want?" she demanded, suspiciously.

"Save me!" cried Phil, out of breath. "Someone is chasing me. He is bad. He will beat me.

The woman's sympathies were quickly enlisted. She had a warm heart, and was always ready to give aid to the oppressed.

"Whist, darling, run upstairs, and hide under the bed. I'll send him off wid a flea in his ear, whoever he is."

Phil was quick to take the hint. He ran upstairs, and concealed himself as directed. While he was doing it, the lower door, which he had shut, was opened by Pietro. He was about to rush into the house, but the muscular form of Phil's friend stood in his way.

"Out wid ye!" said she, flourishing a broom, which she had snatched up. "Is that the way you inter a dacint woman's house, ye spalpeen!"

"I want my brother," said Pietro, drawing back a little before the amazon who disputed his passage.

"Go and find him, thin!" said Bridget McGuire, "and kape out of my house."

"But he is here," said Pietro, angrily; "I saw him come in."

"Then, one of the family is enough," said Bridget. "I don't want another. Lave here wid you!"

"Give me my brother, then!" said Pietro, provoked.

"I don't know anything of your brother. If he looks like you, he's a beauty, sure," returned Mrs. McGuire.

"Will you let me look for him?"

"Faith and I won't. You may call him if you plase."

Pietro knew that this would do very little good, but there seemed nothing else to do.

"Filippo!" he called; "come here. The padrone has sent for you."

"What was ye sayin'?" demanded Bridget not comprehending the Italian.

"I told my brother to come."

"Then you can go out and wait for him," said she. "I don't want you in the house."

Pietro was very angry. He suspected that Phil was in the rear room, and was anxious to search for him. But Bridget McGuire was in the way—no light, delicate woman, but at least forty pounds heavier than Pietro. Moreover, she was armed with a broom, and seemed quite ready to use it. Phil was fortunate in obtaining so able a protector. Pietro looked at her, and had a vague thought of running by her, and dragging Phil out if he found him. But Bridget was planted so squarely in his path that this course did not seem very practicable.

"Will you give me my brother?" demanded Pietro, forced to use words where he would willingly have used blows.

"I haven't got your brother."

"He is in this house."

"Thin he may stay here, but you shan't," said Bridget, and she made a sudden demonstration with the broom, of so threatening a character that Pietro hastily backed out of the house, and the door was instantly bolted in his face.

CHAPTER XXI

THE SIEGE

When the enemy had fairly been driven out of the house Mrs. McGuire went upstairs in search of Phil. Our hero had come out from his place of concealment, and stood at the window.

"Where is Pietro?" he asked, as his hostess appeared in the chamber.

"I drove him out of the house," said Bridget, triumphantly.

"Then he won't come up here?" interrogated Phil.

"It's I that would like to see him thry it," said Mrs. McGuire, shaking her head in a very positive manner, "I'd break my broom over his back first."

Phil breathed freer. He saw that he was rescued from immediate danger.

"Where is he now?"

"He's outside watching for you. He'll have to wait till you come out."

"May I stay here till he goes?"

"Sure, and you may," said the warm-hearted Irishwoman. "You're as welcome as flowers in May. Are you hungry?"

"No, thank you," said Phil. "I have eaten my dinner."

"Won't you try a bit of bread and cold mate now?" she asked, hospitably.

"You are very kind," said Phil, gratefully, "but I am not hungry. I only want to get away from Pietro."

"Is that the heathen's name? Sure I never heard it before."

"It is Peter in English."

"And has he got the name of the blessed St. Peter, thin? Sure, St. Peter would be mightily ashamed of him. And is he your brother, do you say?"

"No," said Phil.

"He said he was; but I thought it was a wicked lie when he said it. He's too bad, sure, to be a brother of yours. But I must go down to my work. My clothes are in the tub, and the water will get cold."

"Will you be kind enough to tell me when he goes away?" asked Phil.

"Sure I will. Rest aisy, darlint. He shan't get hold of you."

Pietro's disappointment may be imagined when he found that the victim whom he had already considered in his grasp was snatched from him in the very moment of his triumph. He felt nearly as much incensed at Mrs. McGuire as at Phil, but against the former he had no remedy. Over the stalwart Irishwoman neither he nor the padrone had any jurisdiction, and he was compelled to own himself ignominiously repulsed and baffled. Still all was not lost. Phil must come out of the house some time, and when he did he would capture him. When that happy moment arrived he resolved to inflict a little punishment on our hero on his own account, in anticipation of that which awaited him from his uncle, the padrone. He therefore took his position in front of the house, and maintained a careful watch, that Phil might not escape unobserved.

So half an hour passed. He could hear no noise inside the house, nor did Phil show himself at any of the windows. Pietro was disturbed by a sudden suspicion. What if, while he was watching, Phil had escaped by the back door, and was already at a distance!

This would be quite possible, for as he stood he could only watch the front of the house. The rear was hidden from his view. Made uneasy by this thought, he shifted his ground, and crept stealthily round on the side, in the hope of catching a view of Phil, or perhaps hearing some conversation between him and his Amazonian protector by which he might set at rest his suddenly formed suspicions.

He was wrong, however. Phil was still upstairs. He was disposed to be cautious, and did not mean to leave his present place of security until he should be apprised by his hostess that Pietro had gone.

Bridget McGuire kept on with her washing. She had been once to the front room, and, looking through the blinds, had ascertained that Pietro was still there.

"He'll have to wait long enough," she said to herself, "the haythen! It's hard he'll find it to get the better of Bridget McGuire."

She was still at her tub when through the opposite window on the side of the house she caught sight of Pietro creeping stealthily along, as we have described.

"I'll be even wid him," said Bridget to herself exultingly. "I'll tache him to prowl around my house."

She took from her sink near by a large, long-handled tin dipper, and filled it full of warm suds from the tub. Then stealing to the window, she opened it suddenly, and as Pietro looked up, suddenly launched the contents in his face, calling forth a volley of imprecations, which I would rather not transfer to my page. Being in Italian, Bridget did not exactly understand their meaning, but guessed it.

"Is it there ye are?" she said, in affected surprise.

"Why did you do that?" demanded Pietro, finding enough English to express his indignation.

"Why did I do it?" repeated Bridget. "How would I know that you were crapin' under my windy? It serves ye right, anyhow. I don't want you here."

"Send out my brother, then," said Pietro.

"There's no brother of yours inside," said Mrs. McGuire.

"It's a lie!" said Pietro, angrily stamping his foot.

"Do you want it ag'in?" asked Bridget, filling her dipper once more from the tub, causing Pietro to withdraw hastily to a greater distance. "Don't you tell Bridget McGuire that she lies."

"My brother is in the house," reiterated Pietro, doggedly.

"He is no brother of yours—he says so."

"He lies," said Pietro.

"Shure and it's somebody else lies, I'm thinkin'," said Bridget.

"Is he in the house?" demanded Pietro, finding it difficult to argue with Phil's protector.

"I don't see him," said Bridget, shrewdly, turning and glancing round the room.

"I'll call the police," said Pietro, trying to intimidate his adversary.

"I wish you would," she answered, promptly. "It would save me the trouble. I'll make a charge against you for thryin' to break into my house; maybe you want to stale something."

Mrs. McGuire flings dippers of hot water down on Pietro while he's creeping under her windows to look for Phil.

Pietro was getting disgusted. Mrs. McGuire proved more unmanageable than he anticipated. It was tantalizing to think that Phil was so near him, and yet out of his reach. He anathematized Phil's protector in his heart, and I am afraid it would have gone hard with her if he could have had his wishes fulfilled. He was not troubled to think what next to say, for Bridget suddenly terminated the interview by shutting down the window with the remark: "Go away from here! I don't want you lookin' in at my windy."

Pietro did not, however, go away immediately. He moved a little further to the rear, having a suspicion that Phil might escape from the door at the back. While he was watching here, he suddenly heard the front door open, and shut with a loud sound. He ran to the front, thinking that Phil might be taking flight from the street door, but it was only a ruse of Mrs. McGuire, who rather enjoyed tantalizing Pietro. He looked carefully up and down the street, but, seeing nothing of Phil, he concluded he must still be inside. He therefore resumed his watch, but in some perplexity as to where he ought to stand, in order to watch both front and rear. Phil occasionally looked guardedly from the window in the second story, and saw his enemy, but knew that as long as he remained indoors he was safe. It was not very agreeable remaining in the chamber alone, but it was a great deal better than falling into the clutches of Pietro, and he felt fortunate to have found so secure a place of refuge.

Pietro finally posted himself at the side of the house, where he could command a view of both front and rear, and there maintained his stand nearly underneath the window at which his intended prisoner was standing.

As Phil was watching him, suddenly he heard steps, and Bridget McGuire entered the chamber. She bore in her hand the same tin dipper before noticed, filled with steaming hot water. Phil regarded her with some surprise.

"Would you like to see some fun now?" she asked, her face covered by a broad smile.

"Yes," said Phil.

"Open the windy, aisy, so he won't hear."

Phil obeyed directions, and managed not to attract the attention of his besieger below, who chanced at the moment to be looking toward the door in the rear.

"Now," said Bridget, "take this dipper and give him the binifit of it."

"Don't let him see you do it," cautioned his protector.

Phil took the idea and the dipper at once.

Phil, holding the dipper carefully, discharged the contents with such good aim that they drenched the watching Pietro. The water being pretty hot, a howl of pain and rage rose from below, and Pietro danced about frantically. Looking up, he saw no one, for Phil had followed directions and drawn his head in immediately. But Mrs. McGuire, less cautious, looked out directly afterward.

"Will ye go now, or will ye stand jist where I throw the hot water?"

In reply, Pietro indulged in some rather emphatic language, but being in the Italian language, in which he was more fluent, it fell unregarded upon the ears of Mrs. McGuire.

"I told you to go," she said. "I've got some more wather inside."

Pietro stepped back in alarm. He had no disposition to take another warm shower bath, and he had found out to his cost that Bridget McGuire was not a timid woman, or easily frightened.

But he had not yet abandoned the siege. He shifted his ground to the front of the house, and took a position commanding a view of the front door.

CHAPTER XXII

THE SIEGE IS RAISED

Though Phil was the besieged party, his position was decidedly preferable to that of Pietro. The afternoon was passing, and he was earning nothing. He finally uncovered his organ and began to play. A few gathered around him, but they were of that class with whom money is not plenty. So after a while, finding no pennies forthcoming, he stopped suddenly, but did not move on, as his auditors expected him to. He still kept his eyes fixed on Mrs. McGuire's dwelling. He did this so long as to attract observation.

"You'll know the house next time, mister," said a sharp boy.

Pietro was about to answer angrily, when a thought struck him.

"Will you do something for me?" he asked.

"How much?" inquired the boy, suggestively.

"Five cents," answered Pietro, understanding his meaning.

"It isn't much," said the boy, reflectively. "Tell me what you want."

Though Pietro was not much of a master of English, he contrived to make the boy understand that he was to go round to the back door and tell Mrs. McGuire that he, Pietro, was gone. He intended to hide close by, and when Phil came out, as he hoped, on the strength of his disappearance, he would descend upon him and bear him off triumphantly.

Armed with these instructions, the boy went round to the back door and knocked.

Thinking it might be Phil's enemy, Mrs. McGuire went to the door, holding in one hand a dipper of hot suds, ready to use in case of emergency.

"Well, what do you want?" she asked, abruptly, seeing that it was a boy.

"He's gone," said the boy.

"Who's gone?"

"The man with the hand-organ, ma'am."

"And what for do I care?" demanded Bridget, suspiciously.

This was a question the boy could not answer. In fact, he wondered himself why such a message should have been sent. He could only look at her in silence.

"Who told you to tell the man was gone?" asked Bridget, with a shrewdness worthy of a practitioner at the bar.

"The Italian told me."

"Did he?" repeated Bridget, who saw into the trick at once. "He's very kind."

"He didn't want you to know he told me," said the boy, remembering his instructions when it was too late.

Mrs. McGuire nodded her head intelligently.

"True for you," said she. "What did he pay you for tellin' me?"

"Five cents."

"Thin it's five cints lost. Do you want to earn another five cints?"

"Yes," said the boy, promptly.

"Thin do what I tell you."

"What is it?"

"Come in and I'll tell you."

The boy having entered, Mrs. McGuire led him to the front door.

"Now," said she, "when I open the door, run as fast as you can. The man that sint you will think it is another boy, and will run after you. Do ye mind?"

The young messenger began to see the joke, and was quite willing to help carry it out. But even the prospective fun did not make him forgetful of his promised recompense.

"Where's the five cents?" he asked.

"Here," said Bridget, and diving into the depths of a capacious pocket, she drew out five pennies.

"That's all right," said the boy. "Now, open the door."

Bridget took care to make a noise in opening the door, and, as it opened, she said in a loud and exultant voice, "You're all safe now; the man's gone."

"Now run," she said, in a lower voice.

The boy dashed out of the doorway, but Mrs. McGuire remained standing there. She was not much surprised to see Pietro run out from the other side of the house, and prepare to chase the runaway. But quickly perceiving that he was mistaken, he checked his steps, and turning, saw Mrs. McGuire with a triumphant smile on her face.

"Why don't you run?" she said. "You can catch him."

"It isn't my brother," he answered, sullenly.

"I thought you was gone," she said.

"I am waiting for my brother."

"Thin you'll have to wait. You wanted to chate me, you haythen! But Bridget McGuire ain't to be took in by such as you. You'd better lave before my man comes home from his work, or he'll give you lave of absence wid a kick."

Without waiting for an answer, Bridget shut the door, and bolted it—leaving her enemy routed at all points.

In fact Pietro began to lose courage. He saw that he had a determined foe to contend with. He had been foiled thus far in every effort to obtain possession of Phil. But the more difficult the enterprise seemed, the more anxious he became to carry it out successfully. He knew that the padrone would not give him a very cordial reception if he returned without Phil, especially as he would be compelled to admit that he had seen him, and had nevertheless failed to secure him. His uncle would not be able to appreciate the obstacles he had encountered, but would consider him in fault. For this reason he did not like to give up the siege, though he saw little hopes of accomplishing his object. At length, however, he was obliged to raise the siege, but from a cause with which neither Phil nor his defender had anything to do.

The sky, which had till this time been clear, suddenly darkened. In ten minutes rain began to fall in large drops. A sudden shower, unusual at this time of the year, came up, and pedestrians everywhere, caught without umbrellas, fled panic-stricken to the nearest shelter. Twice before, as we know, Pietro had suffered from a shower of warm water. This, though colder, was even more formidable. Vanquished by the forces of nature, Pietro shouldered his instrument and fled incontinently. Phil might come out now, if he chose. His enemy had deserted his post, and the coast was clear.

"That'll make the haythen lave," thought Mrs. McGuire, who, though sorry to see the rain on account of her washing, exulted in the fact that Pietro was caught out in it.

She went to the front door and looked out. Looking up the street, she just caught a glimpse of the organ in rapid retreat. She now unbolted the door, the danger being at an end, and went up to acquaint Phil with the good news.

"You may come down now," she said.

"Is he gone?" inquired Phil.

"Shure he's runnin' up the street as fast as his legs can carry him."

"Thank you for saving me from him," said, Phil, with a great sense of relief at the flight of his enemy.

"Whisht now; I don't nade any thanks. Come down by the fire now."

So Phil went down, and Bridget, on hospitable thoughts intent, drew her only rocking-chair near the stove, and forced Phil to sit down in it. Then she told him, with evident enjoyment, of the trick which Pietro had tried to play on her, and how he had failed.

"He couldn't chate me, the haythen!" she concluded. "I was too smart for the likes of him, anyhow. Where do you live when you are at home?"

"I have no home now," said Phil, with tears in his eyes.

"And have you no father and mother?"

"Yes," said Phil. "They live in Italy."

"And why did they let you go so far away?"

"They were poor, and the padrone offered them money," answered Phil, forced to answer, though the subject was an unpleasant one.

"And did they know he was a bad man and would bate you?"

"I don't think they knew," said Phil, with hesitation. "My mother did not know."

"I've got three childer myself," said Bridget; "they'll get wet comin' home from school, the darlints—but I wouldn't let them go with any man to a far country, if he'd give me all the gowld in the world. And where does that man live that trates you so bad?"

"In New York."

"And does Peter—or whatever the heathen's name is—live there too?"

"Yes, Pietro lives there. The padrone is his uncle, and treats him better than the rest of us. He sent him after me to bring me back."

"And what is your name? Is it Peter, like his?"

"No; my name is Filippo."

"It's a quare name."

"American boys call me Phil."

"That's better. It's a Christian name, and the other isn't. Before I married my man I lived five years at Mrs. Robertson's, and she had a boy they called Phil. His whole name was Philip."

"That's my name in English."

"Then why don't you call it so, instead of Philip-O? What good is the O, anyhow? In my country they put the O before the name, instead of to the tail-end of it. My mother was an O'Connor. But it's likely ivery country has its own ways."

Phil knew very little of Ireland, and did not fully understand Mrs. McGuire's philosophical remarks. Otherwise they might have amused him, as they may possibly amuse my readers.

I cannot undertake to chronicle the conversation that took place between Phil and his hostess. She made numerous inquiries, to some of which he was able to give satisfactory replies, to others not. But in half an hour there was an interruption, and a noisy one. Three stout, freckled-faced children ran in at the back door, dripping as if they had just emerged from a shower-bath. Phil moved aside to let them approach the stove.

Forthwith Mrs. McGuire was engaged in motherly care, removing a part of the wet clothing, and lamenting for the state in which her sturdy offspring had returned. But presently order was restored, and the bustle was succeeded by quiet.

"Play us a tune," said Pat, the oldest.

Phil complied with the request, and played tune after tune, to the great delight of the children, as well as of Mrs. McGuire herself. The result was that when, shortly after, on the storm subsiding, Phil proposed to go, the children clamored to have him stay, and he received such a cordial invitation to stop till the next morning that he accepted, nothing loath. So till the next morning our young hero is provided for.

CHAPTER XXIII

A PITCHED BATTLE

Has my youthful reader ever seen a dog slinking home with downcast look and tall between his legs? It was with very much the same air that Pietro in the evening entered the presence of the padrone. He had received a mortifying defeat, and now he had before him the difficult task of acknowledging it.

"Well, Pietro," said the padrone, harshly, "where is Filippo?"

"He is not with me," answered Pietro, in an embarrassed manner.

"Didn't you see him then?" demanded his uncle, hastily.

For an instant Pietro was inclined to reply in the negative, knowing that the censure he would incur would be less. But Phil might yet be taken—he probably would be, sooner or later, Pietro thought—and then his falsehood would be found out, and he would in consequence lose the confidence of the padrone. So, difficult though it was, he thought it politic to tell the truth.

"Si, signore, I saw him," said he.

"Then why didn't you drag him home?" demanded his uncle, with contracted brow. "Didn't I tell you to bring him home?"

"Si, signore, but I could not."

"Are you not so strong as he, then?" asked the padrone, with a sneer. "Is a boy of twelve more than a match for you, who are six years older?"

"I could kill him with my little finger," said Pietro, stung by this taunt, and for the moment he looked as if he would like to do it.

"Then you didn't want to bring him? Come, you are not too old for the stick yet."

Pietro glowed beneath his dark skin with anger and shame when these words were addressed to him. He would not have cared so much had they been alone, but some of the younger boys were present, and it shamed him to be threatened in their presence.

"I will tell you how it happened," he said, suppressing his anger as well as he could, "and you will see that I was not in fault."

"Speak on, then," said his uncle; but his tone was cold and incredulous.

Pietro told the story, as we know it. It will not be necessary to repeat it. When he had finished, his uncle said, with a sneer, "So you were afraid of a woman. I am ashamed of you."

"What could I do?" pleaded Pietro

"What could you do?" repeated the padrone, furiously; "you could push her aside, run into the house, and secure the boy. You are a coward—afraid of a woman!"

"It was her house," said Pietro. "She would call the police."

"So could you. You could say it was your brother you sought. There was no difficulty. Do you think Filippo is there yet?"

"I do not know."

"To-morrow I will go with you myself," said the padrone. "I see I cannot trust you alone. You shall show me the house, and I will take the boy."

Pietro was glad to hear this. It shifted the responsibility from his shoulders, and he was privately convinced that Mrs. McGuire would prove a more formidable antagonist than the padrone imagined. Whichever way it turned out, he would experience a feeling of satisfaction. If the padrone got worsted, it would show that he, Pietro, need not be ashamed of his defeat. If Mrs. McGuire had to surrender at discretion, he would rejoice in her discomfiture. So, in spite of his reprimand, he went to bed with better spirits than he came home.

The next morning Pietro and the padrone proceeded to Newark, as proposed. Arrived there, the former led his uncle at once to the house of the redoubtable Mrs. McGuire. It will be necessary for us to precede them.

Patrick McGuire was a laborer, and for some months past had had steady work. But, as luck would have it, work ceased for him on the day in which his wife had proved so powerful a protector to Phil. When he came home at night he announced this.

"Niver mind, Pat," said Mrs. McGuire, who was sanguine and hopeful, "we'll live somehow. I've got a bit of money upstairs, and I'll earn something by washing. We won't starve."

"I'll get work ag'in soon, maybe," said Pat, encouraged.

"Shure you will."

"And if I don't, I'll help you wash," said her husband, humorously.

"Shure you'd spoil the clothes," said Bridget, laughing.

In the evening Phil played, and they had a merry time. Mr. McGuire quite forgot that he was out of work, and, seizing his wife by the waist, danced around the kitchen, to the great delight of the children.

The next morning Phil thanked Mrs. McGuire for her kindness, and prepared to go away.

"Why will you go?" asked Bridget, hospitably. "Shure we have room for you. You can pay us a little for your atin', and sleep with the childer."

"I should like it," said Phil, "but——"

"But what?"

"Pietro will come for me."

"And if he does, my Pat will kick him out of doors."

Mr. McGuire was six feet in height, and powerfully made. There was no doubt he could do it if he had the opportunity. But Phil knew that he must go out into the streets and then Pietro might waylay him when he had no protector at hand. He explained his difficulty to Mrs. McGuire, and she proposed that he should remain close at hand all the forenoon; near enough to fly to the house as a refuge, if needful. If Pietro did not appear in that time, he probably would not at all.

Phil agreed to this plan, and accordingly began to play and sing in the neighborhood, keeping a watchful lookout for the enemy. His earnings were small, for the neighborhood was poor. Still, he picked up a few pennies, and his store was increased by a twenty-five cent gift from a passing gentleman. He had just commenced a new tune, being at that time ten rods from the house, when his watchful eyes detected the approach of Pietro, and, more formidable still, the padrone.

He did not stop to finish his tune, but took to his heels. At that moment the padrone saw him. With a cry of exultation, he started in pursuit, and Pietro with him. He thought Phil already in his grasp.

Phil dashed breathless into the kitchen, where Mrs. McGuire was ironing.

"What's the matter?" she asked.

"The padrone—Pietro and the padrone!" exclaimed Phil, pale with affright.

Mrs. McGuire took in the situation at once.

"Run upstairs," she said. "Pat's up there on the bed. He will see they won't take you."

Phil sprang upstairs two steps at a time, and dashed into the chamber. Mr. McGuire was lying on the outside of the bed, peacefully smoking a clay pipe.

"What's the matther?" he asked, repeating his wife's question.

"They have come for me," said Phil.

"Have they?" said Pat. "Then they'll go back, I'm thinkin'. Where are they?"

But there was no need of a reply, as their voices were already audible from below, talking with Mrs. McGuire. The distance was so trifling that they had seen Phil enter the house, and the padrone, having a contempt for the physical powers of woman, followed boldly.

They met Mrs. McGuire at the door.

"What do you want?" she demanded.

"The boy," said the padrone. "I saw him come in here."

"Did ye? Your eyes is sharp thin."

She stood directly in the passage, so that neither could enter without brushing her aside.

"Send him out," said the padrone.

"Faith, and I won't," said Bridget. "He shall stay here as long as he likes."

"I will come in and take him," said the padrone, furiously.

"I wouldn't advise ye to thry it," said Mrs. McGuire, coolly.

"Move aside, woman, or I will make you," said the Italian, angrily.

"I'll stay where I am. Shure, it's my own house, and I have a right to do it."

"Pietro," said the padrone, with sudden thought, "he may escape from the front door. Go round and watch it.

By his sign Bridget guessed what he said, though it was spoken in Italian.

"He won't run away," she said. "I'll tell you where he is, if you want to know."

"Where?" asked the padrone, eagerly.

"He's upstairs, thin."

The padrone would not be restrained any longer. He made a rush forward, and, pushing Mrs. McGuire aside, sprang up the stairs. He would have found greater difficulty in doing this, but Bridget, knowing her husband was upstairs, made little resistance, and contented herself, after the padrone had passed, with intercepting

Pietro, and clutching him vigorously by the hair, to his great discomfort, screaming "Murther!" at the top of her lungs.

The padrone heard the cry, but in his impetuosity he did not heed it. He expected to gain an easy victory over Phil, whom he supposed to be alone in the chamber. He sprang toward him, but had barely seized him by the arm, when the gigantic form of the Irishman appeared, and the padrone found himself in his powerful grasp.

"What business have ye here, you bloody villain?" demanded Pat; "breakin' into an honest man's house, without lave or license. I'll teach you manners, you baste!"

"Give me the boy!" gasped the padrone.

"You can't have him, thin!" said Pat "You want to bate him, you murderin' ould villain!"

"I'll have you arrested," said the padrone, furiously, writhing vainly to get himself free. He was almost beside himself that Phil should be the witness of his humiliation.

"Will you, thin?" demanded Pat. "Thin the sooner you do it the betther. Open the window, Phil!

Phil obeyed, not knowing why the request was made. He was soon enlightened. The Irishman seized the padrone, and, lifting him from the floor, carried him to the window, despite his struggles, and, thrusting him out, let him drop. It was only the second story, and there was no danger of serious injury. The padrone picked himself up, only to meet with another disaster. A passing policeman had heard Mrs. McGuire's cries, and on hearing her account had arrested Pietro, and was just in time to arrest the padrone also, on the charge of forcibly entering the house. As the guardian of the peace marched off with Pietro on one side and the padrone on the other, Mrs. McGuire sat down on a chair and laughed till she cried.

"Shure, they won't come for you again in a hurry, Phil, darlint!" she said. "They've got all they want, I'm thinkin'."

I may add that the pair were confined in the station-house over night, and the next day were brought before a justice, reprimanded and fined.

CHAPTER XXIV

THE DEATH OF GIACOMO

Great was the astonishment at the Italian lodging-house that night when neither the padrone nor Pietro made his appearance. Great was the joy, too, for the nightly punishments were also necessarily omitted, and the boys had no one to pay their money to. There was another circumstance not so agreeable. All the provisions were locked up, and there was no supper for the hungry children. Finally, at half-past eleven, three boys, bolder than the rest, went out, and at last succeeded in obtaining some bread and crackers at an oyster saloon, in sufficient quantities to supply all their comrades. After eating heartily they went to bed, and for one night the establishment ran itself much more satisfactorily to the boys than if the padrone had been present.

An Italian boy selling oysters with his Padrone behind him in a vest. Padrones were common in many industries other than street musicians.

The next morning the boys went out as usual, having again bought their breakfast and dispersed themselves about the city and vicinity, heartily hoping that this state of things might continue. But it was too good to last. When they returned at evening they found their old enemy in command. He looked more ill-tempered and sour than ever, but gave no explanation of his and Pietro's absence, except to say that he had been out of the city on business. He called for the boys' earnings of the day previous, but to their surprise made no inquiries about how they had supplied themselves with supper or breakfast. He felt that his influence over the boys, and the terror which he delighted to inspire in them, would be lessened if they should learn that he had been arrested and punished. The boys were accustomed to look upon him as possessed of absolute power over them, and almost regarded him as above law.

Pietro, too, was silent, partly for the same reasons which influenced the padrone, partly because he was afraid of offending his uncle.

Meanwhile poor Giacomo remained sick. If he had been as robust and strong as Phil, he would have recovered, but he was naturally delicate, and exposure and insufficient food had done their work only too well.

Four days afterward (to advance the story a little) one of the boys came to the padrone in the morning, saying: "Signore padrone, Giacomo is much worse. I think he is going to die."

"Nonsense!" said the padrone, angrily. "He is only pretending to be sick, so that he need not work. I have lost enough by him already."

Nevertheless he went to the little boy's bedside.

Giacomo was breathing faintly. His face was painfully thin, his eyes preternaturally bright. He spoke faintly, but his mind seemed to be wandering.

"Where is Filippo?" he said. "I want to see Filippo."

In this wish the padrone heartily concurred. He, too, would have been glad to see Filippo, but the pleasure would not have been mutual.

"Why do you want to see Filippo?" he demanded, in his customary harsh tone.

Giacomo heard and answered, though unconscious who spoke to him.

"I want to kiss him before I die," he said.

"What makes you think you are going to die?" said the tyrant, struck by the boy's appearance.

"I am so weak," murmured Giacomo. "Stoop down, Filippo. I want to tell you something in your ear."

Moved by curiosity rather than humanity, the padrone stooped over, and Giacomo whispered:

"When you go back to Italy, dear Filippo, go and tell my mother how I died. Tell her not to let my father sell my little brother to a padrone, or he may die far away, as I am dying. Promise me, Filippo."

There was no answer. The padrone did indeed feel a slight emotion of pity, but it was, unhappily, transient. Giacomo did not observe that the question was not answered.

"Kiss me, Filippo," said the dying boy.

One of the boys who stood nearby, with tears in his eyes, bent over and kissed him.

Giacomo smiled. He thought it was Filippo. With that smile on his face, he gave one quick gasp and died—a victim of the padrone's tyranny and his father's cupidity.(1)

(1) It is the testimony of an eminent Neapolitan physician (I quote from Signor Casali, editor of L'Eco d'Italia) that of one hundred Italian children who are sold by their parents into this white slavery, but twenty ever return home; thirty grow up and adopt various occupations abroad, and fifty succumb to maladies produced by privation and exposure.

Death came to Giacomo as a friend. No longer could he be forced out into the streets to suffer cold and fatigue, and at night inhuman treatment and abuse. His slavery was at an end.

We go back now to Phil. Though he and his friends had again gained a victory over Pietro and the padrone, he thought it would not be prudent to remain in Newark any longer. He knew the revengeful spirit of his tyrants, and dreaded the chance of again falling into their hands. He must, of course, be exposed to the risk of capture while plying his vocation in the public streets. Therefore he resisted the invitation of his warm-hearted protectors to make his home with them, and decided to wander farther away from New York.

The next day, therefore, he went to the railway station and bought a ticket for a place ten miles further on. This he decided would be far enough to be safe.

Getting out of the train, he found himself in a village of moderate size. Phil looked around him with interest. He had the fondness, natural to his age, for seeing new places. He soon came to a schoolhouse. It was only a quarter of nine, and some of the boys were playing outside. Phil leaned against a tree and looked on.

Though he was at an age when boys enjoy play better than work or study, he had no opportunity to join in their games.

One of the boys, observing him, came up and said frankly, "Do you want to play with us?"

"Yes," said Phil, brightening up, "I should like to."

"Come on, then."

Phil looked at his fiddle and hesitated.

"Oh, I'll take care of your fiddle for you. Here, this tree is hollow; just put it inside, and nobody will touch it."

Phil needed no second invitation. Sure of the safety of his fiddle, which was all-important to him since it procured for him his livelihood, he joined in the game with zest. It was so simple that he easily understood it. His laugh was as loud and merry as any of the rest, and his face glowed with enjoyment.

It does not take long for boys to become acquainted. In the brief time before the teacher's arrival, Phil became on good terms with the schoolboys, and the one who had first invited him to join them said: "Come into school with us. You shall sit in my seat."

"Will he let me?" asked Phil, pointing to the teacher.

"To be sure he will. Come along."

Phil took his fiddle from its hiding-place in the interior of the tree, and walked beside his companion into the schoolroom.

It was the first time he had ever been in a schoolroom before, and he looked about him with curiosity at the desks, and the maps hanging on the walls. The blackboards, too, he regarded with surprise, not understanding their use.

After the opening exercises were concluded, the teacher, whose attention had been directed to the newcomer, walked up to the desk where he was seated. Phil was a little alarmed, for, associating him with his recollections of the padrone, he did not know but that he would be punished for his temerity in entering without the teacher's invitation.

But he was soon reassured by the pleasant tone in which he was addressed.

"What is your name, my young friend?"

"Filippo."

"You are an Italian, I suppose."

"Si, signore."

"Does that mean 'Yes, sir'?"

"Yes, sir," answered Phil, remembering to speak English.

"Is that your violin?"

"Yes, sir."

"Where do you live?"

Phil hesitated.

"I am traveling," he said at last.

"You are young to travel alone. How long have you been in this country?"

"A year."

"And have you been traveling about all that time?"

"No, signore; I have lived in New York."

"I suppose you have not gone to school?"

"No, signore."

"Well, I am glad to see you here; I shall be glad to have you stay and listen to our exercises."

The teacher walked back to his desk, and the lessons began. Phil listened with curiosity and attention. For the first time in his life he felt ashamed of his own ignorance, and wished he, too, might have a chance to learn, as the children around him were doing. But they had homes and parents to supply their wants, while he must work for his livelihood.

After a time, recess came. Then the boys gathered around, and asked Phil to play them a tune.

"Will he let me?" asked the young fiddler, again referring to the teacher.

The latter, being applied to, readily consented, and expressed his own wish to hear Phil. So the young minstrel played and sang several tunes to the group of children who gathered around him. Time passed rapidly, and the recess was over before the children anticipated it.

"I am sorry to disturb your enjoyment," said the teacher; "but duty before pleasure, you know. I will only suggest that, as our young friend here depends on his violin for support, we ought to collect a little money for him. James Reynolds, suppose you pass around your hat for contributions. Let me suggest that you come to me first."

The united offerings, though small individually, amounted to a dollar, which Phil pocketed with much satisfaction. He did not remain after recess, but resumed his wanderings, and about noon entered a grocery store, where he made a hearty lunch. Thus far good fortune attended him, but the time was coming, and that before long, when life would wear a less sunny aspect.

CHAPTER XXV

PHIL FINDS A FRIEND

It was the evening before Christmas. Until to-day the winter had been an open one, but about one o'clock in the afternoon the snow began to fall. The flakes came thicker and faster, and it soon became evident that an old-fashioned snowstorm had set in. By seven o'clock the snow lay a foot deep on the level, but in some places considerably deeper, for a brisk wind had piled it up in places.

In a handsome house, some rods back from the village street, lived Dr. Drayton, a physician, whose skill was so well appreciated that he had already, though still in the prime of life, accumulated a handsome competence.

He sat this evening in his library, in dressing-gown and slippers, his wife nearby engaged in some needlework.

"I hope you won't be called out this evening, Joseph," said Mrs. Drayton, as a gust of wind tattled the window panes.

"I echo that wish, my dear," said the doctor, looking up from the last number of the Atlantic Monthly. "I find it much more comfortable here, reading Dr. Holmes' last article."

"The snow must be quite deep."

"It is. I found my ride from the north village this afternoon bleak enough. You know how the wind sweeps across the road near the Pond schoolhouse. I believe there is to be a Christmas-eve celebration in the Town Hall this evening, is there not?"

"No; it has been postponed till to-morrow evening."

"That will be better. The weather and walking will both be better. Shall we go, Mary?"

"If you wish it," she said, hesitatingly.

Her husband understood her hesitation. Christmas day was a sad anniversary for them. Four years before, their only son, Walter, a boy of eight, had died just as the Christmas church bells were ringing out a summons to church. Since then the house had been a silent one, the quiet unbroken by childish noise and merriment. Much as the doctor and his wife were to each other, both felt the void which Walter's death had created, and especially as the anniversary came around which called to mind their great loss.

"I think we had better go," said the doctor; "though God has bereft us of our own child, it will be pleasant for us to watch the happy faces of others."

"Perhaps you are right, Joseph."

Half an hour passed. The doctor continued reading the Atlantic, while his wife, occupied with thoughts which the conversation had called up, kept on with her work.

Just then the bell was heard to ring.

"I hope it is not for you, Joseph," said his wife, apprehensively.

"I am afraid it is," said the doctor, with a look of resignation.

"I thought it would be too good luck for me to have the whole evening to myself."

"I wish you were not a doctor," said Mrs. Drayton.

"It is rather too late to change my profession, my dear," said her husband, good-humoredly. "I shall be fifty next birthday. To be sure, Ellen Jones tells me that in her class at the Normal School there is a maiden lady of sixty-two, who has just begun to prepare herself for the profession of a teacher. I am not quite so old as that."

Here the servant opened the door, ushering in a farm laborer.

"Good-evening, Abner," said the doctor, recognizing him, as, indeed, he knew every face within half a dozen miles. "Anything amiss at home?"

"Mrs. Felton is took with spasms," said Abner. "Can you come right over?"

"What have you done for her?"

"Put her feet in warm water, and put her to bed. Can you come right over?"

"Yes," said the doctor, rising and exchanging his dressing gown for a coat, and drawing on his boots. "I will go as soon as my horse is ready."

Orders were sent out to put the horse to the sleigh. This was quickly done, and the doctor, fully accoutered, walked to the door.

"I shall be back as soon as I can, Mary," he said.

"That won't be very soon. It is a good two-miles' ride."

"I shan't loiter on the way, you may be sure of that. Abner, I am ready."

The snow was still falling, but not quite so fast as early in the afternoon. The wind, however, blew quite as hard, and the doctor found all his wrappings needful.

At intervals on the road he came to deep drifts of snow through which the horse had some difficulty in drawing the sleigh, but at length he arrived at the door of his patient. He found that the violence of her attack was over, and, satisfied of this, left a few simple directions, which he considered sufficient. Nature would do the rest.

"Now for home!" he said to himself. "I hope this will be my last professional call this evening. Mary will be impatient for my return."

He gave the reins to his horse, who appeared to feel that he was bound homeward, and traveled with more alacrity than he had come.

He, too, no doubt shared the doctor's hope that this was the last service required of him before the morrow.

Doctor Drayton had completed rather more than half his journey, when, looking to the right, his attention was drawn to a small, dark object, nearly covered with snow.

Instinctively he reined up his horse.

"Good heavens!" he exclaimed, "it must be a boy. God grant he is not frozen!"

The Doctor goes out into the snow in his sleigh to help a patient. On his way back home, he finds Phil buried in a snowdrift.

He leaped from his sleigh, and lifted the insensible body.

"It is an Italian boy, and here is his violin. The poor child may be dead," he said to himself in a startled tone. "I must carry him home, and see what I can do for him."

So he took up tenderly our young hero—for our readers will have guessed that it was Phil—and put both him and his violin into the sleigh. Then he drove home with a speed which astonished even his horse, who, though anxious to reach his comfortable stable, would not voluntarily have put forth so great an exertion as was now required of him.

I must explain that Phil had for the last ten days been traveling about the country, getting on comfortably while the ground was bare of snow. To-day, however, had proved very uncomfortable. In the city the snow would have been cleared off, and would not have interfered so much with traveling.

He had bought some supper at a grocery store, and, after spending an hour there, had set out again on his wanderings. He found the walking so bad that he made up his mind to apply for a lodging at a house not far back; but a fierce dog, by his barking, had deterred him from the application. The road was lonely, and he had seen no other house since. Finally, exhausted by the effort of dragging himself through the deep snow, and, stiff with cold, he sank down by the side of the road, and would doubtless have frozen had not the doctor made his appearance opportunely.

Mrs. Drayton was alarmed when her husband entered the sitting-room, bearing Phil's insensible form.

She jumped to her feet in alarm.

"Who is it, Joseph?" she asked.

"A poor Italian boy, whom I found by the side of the road."

"Is he dead?" asked the doctor's wife, quickly.

"I think not. I will restore him if there is any life left in him."

It was fortunate for Phil that he had been discovered by a skillful physician, who knew the most effectual means of bringing him to. The flame of life was burning low, and a little longer exposure would have closed the earthly career of our young hero. But he was spared, as we hope, for a happy and useful career.

By the application of powerful restoratives Phil was at length brought round. His chilled limbs grew warm, and his heart began to beat more steadily and strongly. A bed was brought down to the sitting-room, and he was placed in it.

"Where am I?" he asked faintly, when he opened his eyes.

"You are with friends, my boy. Don't ask questions now. In the morning, you may ask as many as you like."

Phil closed his eyes languidly, and soon fell into a sound sleep.

Nature was doing her work well and rapidly.

In the morning Phil woke up almost wholly restored.

As he opened his eyes, he met the kind glances of the doctor and his wife.

"How do you feel this morning?" asked the doctor.

"I feel well," said Phil, looking around him with curiosity.

"Do you think you could eat some breakfast?" asked Dr. Drayton, with a smile.

"Yes, sir," said Phil.

"Then, my lad, I think I can promise you some as soon as you are dressed. But I see from your looks you want to know where you are and how you came here. Don't you remember the snow-storm yesterday?"

Phil shuddered. He remembered it only too well.

"I found you lying by the side of the road about half-past eight in the evening. I suppose you don't remember my picking you up?"

"No, sir."

"You were insensible. I was afraid at first you were frozen. But I brought you home, and, thanks to Providence, you are all right again."

"Where is my fiddle?" asked Phil, anxiously.

"It is safe. There it is on the piano."

Phil was relieved to see that his faithful companion was safe. He looked upon it as his stock in trade, for without it he would not have known how to make his livelihood.

He dressed quickly, and was soon seated at the doctor's well-spread table. He soon showed that, in spite of his exposure and narrow escape from death, he had a hearty appetite. Mrs. Drayton saw him eat with true motherly pleasure, and her natural love of children drew her toward our young hero, and would have done so even had he been less attractive.

"Joseph," she said, addressing her husband, "I want to speak to you a moment."

He followed her out of the room.

"Well, my dear?" he said.

"I want to ask a favor."

"It is granted in advance."

"Perhaps you will not say so when you know what it is."

"I can guess it. You want to keep this boy."

"Are you willing?"

"I would have proposed it, if you had not. He is without friends and poor. We have enough and to spare. We will adopt him in place of our lost Walter."

"Thank you, Joseph. It will make me happy. Whatever I do for him, I will do for my lost darling."

They went back into the room. They found Phil with his cap on and his fiddle under his arm.

"Where are you going, Philip?" asked the doctor.

"I am going into the street. I thank you for your kindness."

"Would you not rather stay with us?"

Phil looked up, uncertain of his meaning.

"We had a boy once, but he is dead. Will you stay with us and be our boy?"

Phil looked in the kind faces of the doctor and his wife, and his face lighted up with joy at the unexpected prospect of such a home, with people who would be kind to him.

"I will stay," he said. "You are very kind to me."

So our little hero had drifted into a snug harbor. His toils and privations were over. And for the doctor and his wife it was a glad day also. On Christmas Day four years before they had lost a child. On this Christmas, God had sent them another to fill the void in their hearts.

CHAPTER XXVI

CONCLUSION

It was a strange thing for the homeless fiddler to find himself the object of affectionate care and solicitude—to feel, when he woke up in the morning, no anxiety about the day's success. He could not have found a better home. Naturally attractive, and without serious faults, Phil soon won his way to the hearts of the good doctor and his wife. The house seemed brighter for his presence, and the void in the heart of the bereaved mother was partially filled. Her lost Walter would have been of the same age as Phil, had he lived. For his sake she determined to treat the boy, who seemed cast by Providence upon her protection, as a son.

To begin with, Phil was carried to the village tailor, where an ample wardrobe was ordered for him. His old clothes were not cast aside, but kept in remembrance of his appearance at the time he came to them. It was a novel sensation for Phil, when, in his new suit, with a satchel of books in his hand, he set out for the town school. It is needless to say that his education was very defective, but he was far from deficient in natural ability, and the progress he made was so rapid that in a year he was on equal footing with the average of boys at his age. He was able at that time to speak English as fluently as his companions, and, but for his dark eyes, and clear brown complexion, he might have been mistaken for an American boy.

His popularity with his schoolfellows was instant and decided. His good humor and lively disposition might readily account for that, even if his position as the adopted son of a prominent citizen had no effect. But it was understood that the doctor, who had no near relatives, intended to treat Phil in all respects as a son, even to leaving him his heir.

It may be asked whether the padrone gave up all efforts to recover the young fiddler. He was too vindictive for this. Boys had run away from him before, but none had subjected him to such ignominious failure in the effort for their recovery. It would have fared ill with our young hero if he had fallen again into the hands of his unscrupulous enemy. But the padrone was not destined to recover him. Day after day Pietro explored the neighboring towns, but all to no purpose. He only visited the principal towns, while Phil was in a small town, not likely to attract the attention of his pursuers.

A week after his signal failure in Newark, the padrone inserted an advertisement in the New York Herald, offering a reward of twenty-five dollars for the recovery of Phil. But our hero was at that time wandering about the country, and the advertisement did not fall under the eyes of those with whom he came in contact. At length the padrone was compelled to own himself baffled and give up the search. He was not without hopes, however, that sometime Phil would turn up. He did hear of him again through Pietro, but not in a way to bring him any nearer his recovery.

This is the way it happened:

One Saturday morning in March, about three months after Phil had found a home, the doctor said to him: "Phil, I am going to New York this morning on a little business; would you like to come with me?"

Phil's eyes brightened. Though he was happy in his village home, he had longed at times to find himself in the city streets with which his old vagabond life had rendered him so familiar.

"I should like it very much," he answered, eagerly.

"Then run upstairs and get ready. I shall start in fifteen minutes."

Phil started, and then turned back.

"I might meet Pietro, or the padrone," he said, hesitating.

"No matter if you do, I shall be with you. If they attempt to recover you, I will summon the police."

The doctor spoke so confidently that Phil dismissed his momentary fear. Two hours later they set foot in New York.

"Now, Phil," said the doctor, "my business will not take long. After that, if there are any friends you would like to see, I will go with you and find them."

"I should like to see Paul Hoffman," said Phil. "I owe him two dollars and a half for the fiddle."

"He shall be paid," said the doctor. "He shall lose nothing by trusting you."

An hour afterward, while walking with the doctor in a side street, Phil's attention was attracted by the notes of a hand-organ. Turning in the direction from which they came, he met the glance of his old enemy, Pietro.

"It is Pietro," he said, quickly, touching the arm of his companion.

Pietro had not been certain till then that it was Phil. It looked like him, to be sure, but his new clothing and general appearance made such a difference between him and the Phil of former days that he would have supposed it only an accidental resemblance. But Phil's evident recognition of him convinced him of his identity. He instantly ceased playing, and, with eager exultation, advanced to capture him. Phil would have been alarmed but for his confidence in the doctor's protection.

"I have got you at last, scelerato," said Pietro, roughly, grasping Phil by the shoulder with a hostile glance.

The doctor instantly seized him by the collar, and hurled him back.

"What do you mean by assaulting my son?" he demanded, coolly.

Pietro was rather astonished at this unexpected attack.

"He is my brother," he said. "He must go back with me."

"He is not your brother. If you touch him again, I will hand you to the police."

"He ran away from my uncle," said Pietro.

"Your uncle should have treated him better."

"He stole a fiddle," said Pietro, doggedly.

"He had paid for it over and over again," said the doctor. "Phil, come along. We have no further business with this young man."

They walked on, but Pietro followed at a little distance. Seeing this, Dr. Drayton turned back.

"Young man," he said, "do you see that policeman across the street?"

"Si, signore," answered Pietro.

"Then I advise you to go in a different direction, or I shall request him to follow you."

Pietro's sallow face was pale with rage. He felt angry enough to tear Phil to pieces, but his rage was unavailing. He had a wholesome fear of the police, and the doctor's threat was effectual. He turned away, though with reluctance, and Phil breathed more freely. Pietro communicated his information to the padrone, and the latter, finding that Phil had found a powerful protector, saw that it would be dangerous for him to carry the matter any further, and sensibly resolved to give up the chase.

Of the padrone I have only further to say that some months later he got into trouble. In a low drinking saloon an altercation arose between him and another ruffian one evening, when the padrone, in his rage, drew a knife, and stabbed his adversary. He was arrested and is now serving out his sentence in Sing Sing.

Pietro, by arrangement with him, took his place, stipulating to pay him a certain annual sum. But he has taken advantage of his uncle's incarceration to defraud him, and after the first payment neglected to make any returns. It may readily be imagined that this imbitters the padrone's imprisonment. Knowing what I do of his fierce temper, I should not be surprised to hear of a murderous encounter between him and his nephew after his release from imprisonment, unless, as is probable, just before the release, Pietro should flee the country with the ill-gotten gains he may have acquired during his term of office. Meanwhile the boys are treated with scarcely less rigor by him than by his uncle, and toil early and late, suffering hardships and privations, that Pietro may grow rich.

Paul Hoffman had often thought of Phil, and how he had fared. He was indeed surprised and pleased when the young fiddler walked up and called him by name.

"Phil," he exclaimed, grasping his hand heartily, "I am very glad to see you. Have you made a fortune?"

"He has found a father," said Dr. Drayton, speaking for Phil, "who wants to thank you for your past kindness to his son."

"It was nothing," said Paul, modestly.

"It was a great deal to Phil, for, except your family, he had no friends."

To this Paul made a suitable reply, and gave Phil and his new father an earnest invitation to dine with him. This the doctor declined, but agreed to call at the rooms of Mrs. Hoffman, if Paul would agree to come and pass the next Sunday with Phil as his visitor. Paul accepted the invitation with pleasure, and it is needless to say that he received a hearty welcome and agreed, in the approaching summer, to make another visit.

And now we bid farewell to Phil, the young, street musician. If his life henceforth shall be less crowded with adventures, and so less interesting, it is because he has been fortunate in securing a good home. Some years hence the Doctor promises to give himself a vacation, and take Phil with him to Europe, where he will seek out his Italian home, and the mother with whom he has already opened communication by letter. So we leave Phil in good hands, and with the prospect of a prosperous career. But there are hundreds of young street musicians who have not met with his good fortune, but are compelled, by hard necessity, to submit to the same privations and hardships from which he is happily relieved. May a brighter day dawn for them also!

I hope my readers feel an interest in Paul Hoffman, the young street merchant, who proved so efficient a friend to our young hero. His earlier adventures are chronicled in "Paul, the Peddler." His later history will be chronicled in the next volume of this series, which will be entitled "Slow and Sure; or From the Sidewalk to the Shop."

THE END

~ ~ ~

TEACHERS GUIDE QUESTIONS FOR PHIL THE FIDDLER

1. How has Phil come to be owned by the Padrone?
2. Phil has skills and qualities that make him more successful than the other boys. What are they?
3. Phil takes care of his friend Giacomo, sometimes at the expense of his own needs. Why does he do this?
4. Why does the Padrone have so much power over the boys? Why don't they go to the police to report his crimes?
5. Tim Rafferty steals Phil's fiddle and breaks it. Was this a blessing in disguise? Why or why not?
6. Phil meets Paul Hoffman many times during this story. What lesson does Paul Hoffman have for Phil?
7. This story refers to Phil's situation as white slavery. Do you agree that it's slavery? Why or why not?
8. Based on the story, how do the citizens of New York feel about the street musicians? Would people change their opinion if the new about how they lived?
9. Phil manages to survive in this story thanks to the charity of others. Who helps Phil, and why do they do it? What message is the author trying to tell here?

TEACHERS GUIDE ANSWERS FOR PHIL THE FIDDLER

1. Phil comes to be owned by the Padrone because his father sold him to him for $100.
2. First, Phil can speak some English, which goes a long way with the people in New York City. Phil also has a very positive personality, which draws people towards him.
3. Phil helps Giacomo because they are friends, and even grew up in the same village in Calabria. Giacomo is weaker than Phil, so Phil feels that he is Giacomo's protector.
4. The Padrone has so much power over the boys because he beats them when they disobey. They boys, most of them who don't speak English, know nothing of the laws in the United States, and therefore feel that there is nothing that can be done to free them from the Padrone.
5. It was a blessing in disguise for Tim to steal Phil's fiddle, because it finally gave Phil a reason to run away from the Padrone.
6. Paul's message for Phil is that he'll get away from the Padrone someday. He also says that with enough hard work, Phil will become rich in America.
7. Phil's situation is absolutely slavery. The boys are sold into service and "owned" by their Padrone as if they were property. When they don't perform up to expectations, they are beaten.
8. Not knowing their plight, many of the citizens of New York treat the street musicians as if they are a nuisance. Some people don't hesitate to call the street musicians thieves, and they have a lack of patience for the boys who don't know English. While it's hard to say what they would think if they knew about their living situation, New Yorkers had plenty of sympathy for black slaves during the civil war, and it's to be expected that they would share the same sympathy for white slaves.
9. Paul helps Phil because he knew what it meant to be poor. The Irish woman in Newark helps Phil because she feels sorry for him, and knows that Pietro is up to no good. Finally, the doctor and his wife adopt Phil because they found him on the anniversary of their own son's death. The author depicts Phil as not being able to survive without charity because he's stressing how important it is that we all take care of each other.

THE LIFE AND THEMES OF
HORATIO ALGER, JR.

By Stefan Kanfer

The Merriam-Webster Dictionary devotes one sentence to him: "Of, relating to, or resembling the fiction of Horatio Alger in which success is achieved through self-reliance and hard work."

True as far as it goes, but that sentence reveals nothing about the man or his accomplishment. Then again, other contemporary reference books are just as terse. Not one acknowledges that Alger in his day (circa 1880-1920) was a publishing phenomenon. During those decades, when a sale of 10,000 volumes was deemed a triumph, readers bought more than 200 million copies of Alger's works, placing him in a league with J.K. Rowling and Stephen King.

Alas, today most of his novels—and there are more than 100—are out of print. But not for long. Thanks to the resuscitation efforts of Sumner Books, a division of Creators Syndicate, Alger's best literary productions are being furnished with fresh covers, new fonts and energetic promotion.

Seldom has there been a more relevant illustration of the maxim that what goes around comes around. At the turn of the 19th century, Alger was the standard-bearer of a phenomenally successful experiment in social reform and personal improvement. That movement inspired disadvantaged kids to move on up, leading juvenile delinquents into productive, significant lives. Men as different as Groucho Marx and Ernest Hemingway were fans.

"Horatio Alger's books conveyed a powerful message to me," wrote Marx, "and to many of my young friends as well—that if you worked hard at your trade, the big chance would eventually come. As a child I didn't regard it as a myth, and as an old man I think of it as the story of my life."

Hemingway's sister Marcelline recalled that during their childhood, "There was one summer when Ernest couldn't get enough of Horatio Alger." Not that Alger's boys' books influenced Papa's prose style. But there must have been something in the writer's stress on grit and self-reliance that affected young Ernest, as it did so many of his contemporaries.

By the end of the Roaring Twenties, though, Horatio Alger had become as passé as the Ford Model T. During the Depression he fared no better; Nathaniel West's satirical 1934 novel, A Cool Million, sent Alger's plots in reverse, as the naïve protagonist loses limb after limb seeking success among rapacious capitalists. Decades later, the film adaptation of Hunter Thompson's 1971 novel, Fear and Loathing in Las Vegas, presented the antihero as "Horatio Alger gone mad on drugs in Las Vegas."

What lay behind Alger's ability to enchant so many Americans—and to enrage so many others? The author's story furnishes a trove of clues:

The sickly child of a Unitarian minister in Marlborough, Massachusetts, Horatio, born in 1832, was always the smallest in his class and far from an academic star. Still, his report cards were good enough for admission to Harvard. There his academic prowess was in inverse proportion to his size (5 feet 2 inches). He won prizes, published verse and fiction in undergraduate magazines, and labeled the entire four years a period of "unmixed happiness."

Decades would pass before he found such contentment again. Upon graduation, Horatio attempted to make his way as a writer. After five unsuccessful years, he returned to Harvard, this time to study at the Divinity School. In 1860 the Reverend Horatio Alger was named minister of the First Parish Unitarian Church of Brewster on Cape Cod. Salary: $800 per year. To supplement his meager income, he turned once again to writing. This time, his stories were well-received, and he allowed himself to dream of a dual career of preacher and writer. That's when catastrophe struck.

It was of his own making, if one historian is to be believed. According to this claim, a 13-year-old told his parents that the new parson had made advances to him. An investigation began. Another lad made a similar complaint. Faced with charges of behaving inappropriately, the accused was allowed to resign—with the proviso that he leave town at once.

Sometime later, Horatio wrote a poem about one Friar Anselmo, who had committed an unspecified crime. Melancholy and remorseful, he comes across a wounded traveler and gives him aid. Whereupon an angel materializes and offers salvation:

> Thy guilty stains shall be washed white again
> By noble service done thy fellow man.

The fugitive repaired to New York City in the spring of 1866, resolved to live out the Christian ideal, expiating his sin by saving others. The Manhattan he entered was the epicenter of the Gilded Age, a magnet for millions of ambitious climbers, drawn by the post-Civil War boom. Out of sight of the glittering prosperity, the mansions and carriages, however, was another New York, a squalid night town that travelers compared to Calcutta, India.

In The Good Old Days, They Were Terrible, historian Otto Bettmann reports that there was scarcely a slum that pedestrians could negotiate "without climbing over a heap of trash or, in rain, wading through a bed of slime." Many streets were so dangerous that policemen hesitated to walk them alone. A Gramercy Park resident noted in his diary, "Most of my friends are investing in revolvers and carry them about at night"—and the Park was one of the city's better neighborhoods.

The New York City street urchin entered the national consciousness in those years. More than 60,000 neglected or abandoned kids ran unsupervised in the street, partly because of the fallout from the tidal waves of immigration from Europe and partly because of families broken by the Civil War.

What was to be done about these juveniles likely to die on the streets or to end up behind bars? The Reverend Charles Loring Brace founded the Children's Aid Society, designed to take homeless or abused kids away from their corrosive environments. At the same time, John Hughes, New York's first Roman Catholic archbishop, set up parochial schools and a residential institution called the Catholic Protectory, which brought up abandoned or orphaned children to be useful members of society.

Horatio Alger joined these efforts at reclamation. He, too, asked himself what could be done about homeless children. Seeking answers, he wandered through the city's worst neighborhoods. He interviewed "street arabs" who spoke of broken homes, violent confrontations with parents, doomed futures. He observed how their cocky attitudes masked a profound despair. He advised them to get real jobs instead of hanging about, squandering whatever came their way from shining shoes or picking pockets. A handful nodded in agreement, expressing the desire to change their lives; most were content to take life as they found it.

Why, he pondered, did individuals subjected to the same conditions turn out so differently? One boy might become a thief, a sociopath, even a killer. His neighbor, perhaps his brother, might aim to be an upright citizen. What was the difference between them?

What saved certain boys, he came to believe, was a quality that gave them the strength to resist sloth and temptation. In a word, character. But was this inborn? In that case determinism won the day, and change was out of the question. Or, given the right opportunity and attitude, could a dispossessed youth win his share of the American dream? The latter, Alger believed—but only if the boy stopped regarding himself as a victim.

As Alger meditated upon the worst crime of the slums—the stealing of childhood from children—an idea came to him. He would be Brother Anselmo redivivus. He had sinned against youths; now he would rescue them—and in the process save himself. As the novelist put it, by depicting the situation of city waifs, he would "excite a deeper and more widespread sympathy in the public mind, as well as exert a salutary influence upon the class of whom he is writing, by setting before them inspiring examples of what energy, ambition, and an honest purpose may achieve."

Ragged Dick became the template of the fiction to follow. Subtitled Street Life in New York with the Boot Blacks, it charted the rise of a 14-year-old boy from poverty to prosperity. Dick Hunter is an adolescent with all odds against him. He has no family, he smokes, drinks alcohol when he can afford it—not very often on the small change he gets from shining gentlemen's shoes—and sleeps on gratings in the winter.

Yet something separates him from his fellow waifs. He refuses to pick pockets like the others, won't mock his elders, and yearns to "grow up 'spectable.'" His bearing and his innate decency attract the attention of upright New Yorkers. One introduces him to his church; another presents Dick with a few dollars.

The earnest youth resolves to become literate to save his money and live a clean life. One day on a walk near South Ferry he sees a toddler fall in the water. Without hesitation, Dick jumps in and saves the drowning child. In gratitude, the father, an affluent businessman, offers the rescuer a job in his office. Gainfully employed, the onetime vagabond Dick Hunter becomes Richard Hunter Esq., and shuts the door forever on the "old vagabond life which he hoped never to resume."

Naïve? Simplistic? To the jaded, the cynical and the ignorant, yes. But not to thousands of children trapped in the real world of poverty and early death. They got the message of Ragged Dick and demanded more Horatio Alger novels with more moral lessons for them to absorb. Those books changed—and in many cases saved—lives a century before Dr. Martin Luther King Jr. stated his belief that what mattered was not the color of one's skin but the content of one's character.

Today, if you listen closely you can hear, amid the jeers, the escalating sound of the last laugh. In 1947, the Horatio Alger Association was founded. It attracts more prominent men and women now than it did then. The group is dedicated to recognizing American leaders who rose, like Alger's young heroes, from humble origins "through honesty, hard work, self-reliance and perseverance." With grants to U.S. high-school students who have "faced and overcome great obstacles in their young lives," the association encourages them to emulate such enterprising and disparate members as Oprah Winfrey and Ray Kroc, Tom Brokaw and Maya Angelou, Stan Musial and Colin Powell.

They can all testify to the truths that lie between the covers of this volume. Turn the first few pages, and you'll understand why so many followed Horatio Alger's breathless, cliff-hanging chapters leading the way from skid row to success. And why so many more are about to read that map in a world where everything has changed—except the basic truths of life.

Stefan Kanfer is an award-winning writer for City Journal and the author of numerous best-selling books.

ABOUT HORATIO ALGER, JR.

Horatio Alger was born in 1832 in Chelsea, Massachusetts. He spent his early years in the small town and under the guidance of the church and his father, the town pastor, before the family moved just west of Boston to the town of Marlborough.

As a shy young boy, Alger poured himself into books and soon became a distinguished student. He studied at Harvard and Harvard Divinity School before becoming a minister. He practiced ministry for a few years near Boston and on Cape Cod, but he was distracted by his true passion: writing.

He loved to write, and by 1865 Alger had written a handful of stories, including Frank's Campaign and Paul Prescott's Charge. The latter was the first in a series of stories that would eventually lead to his great success. In 1866, Alger moved to New York to write poetry, newspaper stories and magazine articles. However, he was shocked to find so many homeless and forgotten children among the streets, an unfortunate consequence of the Civil War. He made it his duty to aid the condition of these lost children, both through his stories and by his continuous acts of benevolence.

Horatio Alger became a household name shortly after the Civil War when he began publishing stories in the form of serializations. These serializations were featured in magazines such as Student and Schoolmate and were later compiled as books. Alger's books became enormously popular, especially among teenage boys across the country, and they soon reached millions and millions of readers. Alger continued to produce several stories a year, and, in later years, wrote novels in and of themselves instead of novels from magazine serials.

The years immediately following the Civil War were the same years when the United States emerged as one nation on the road to becoming a worldwide empire. The years between 1865 and 1900 were the years of the empire builders, with the rags-to-riches stories of John D. Rockefeller, Andrew Carnegie, Cornelius Vanderbilt and Thomas Edison. They were the years that laid the foundation for Henry Ford and other business titans and for the spectacular growth of the American economy throughout the 20th century and through today. During these years, Alger published well over 100 stories, poems and novels that spoke to the timeless themes and successes of this era.

The theme of Alger's books is consistent: If you work hard, go the extra mile, are faithful and honest, show kindness and generosity, and maintain a cheerful, positive and optimistic attitude, you will succeed in creating financial security and happiness. On the other hand, if you lie, cheat, steal, are lazy or envious, and try to take advantage of other people, you will be doomed to failure and misery. Despite his background as a preacher, Alger does not make these points in a self-righteous or pontificating way. What he does instead -- just like the parables that Jesus told -- is to create stories that illustrate the virtues that lead to success. And the stories that Alger creates are no ordinary stories. Each one is filled with lively plots and twists and turns, ones that are always unexpected and keep the reader wanting to know what's going to happen next.

As Alger grew older, he continuously strived to write the Great American Novel, little realizing that the rags-to-riches stories he created were more influential than any other novelists'. He travelled out west in early 1877 searching for new material and returned near the end of the year, producing similar stories with a new western backdrop. By 1897, Alger was suffering from asthma, bronchitis and slight short-term memory loss. He moved in with his sister in South Natick, Massachusetts where he spent the last two years of his life.

Most people have never heard of Horatio Alger while some are vaguely familiar with the term "rags-to-riches." In the Alger family, it was the norm to burn correspondence and manuscripts, and this, coupled with Alger's shyness, has greatly kept him from history's limelight. Though too often forgotten today, Alger's works and the themes within them still affect the American psyche. Many assert that there is a lagging spirit in present American culture, that these inspiring stories are irrelevant. Young people are bombarded with external stimuli that make it difficult for them to get to know themselves. Wide-eyed innocence and childlike enthusiasm, once revered as admirable qualities, are sources of mockery and disdain, which makes cynicism and pessimism inevitable. Video games, television shows, movies and music are all aimed at titillating and at seeing who can be the most gritty, violent or shocking. More than a few commentators have used the word "degrading" to describe the assault that children encounter today.

This is unfortunate. Young people need heroes and role models today just as much as they did in the 1870s and '80s, when Alger was creating them at a feverish pace from his New York City apartment, writing as many as four books at a time. Publisher A.K. Loring asserted that Alger's books "captured the spirits of reborn America" for "above all you can hear the cry of triumph of the oppressed over the oppressor … What Alger has done is to portray the soul – the ambitious soul – of the country." Years later, biographer Edwin P. Hoyt concludes that Alger is "a writer whose influence on the American scene has been so profound that it is hard to measure." Indeed, Alger's works made an overwhelming impression on American culture and society that are still alive with us today. It is for this reason that these classics must be brought to a new generation of readers.

OUR COMMITMENT TO
HORATIO ALGER

By Rick Newcombe

Sumner Books is totally committed to reviving interest in Horatio Alger, one of the best-selling authors of all time yet someone who has been all but forgotten today. I'd like to tell you how this project came about.

Probably the best starting point is to tell you a little about myself. I grew up in suburban Chicago, and my parents were religious and fundamentally optimistic in their outlook on life. They encouraged all eight of their children to be positive in our thinking and hope and pray for the best in all situations. In my adolescence, I discovered many of the self-help authors from the 20th century, including Dale Carnegie, Napoleon Hill and Norman Vincent Peale. I remember reading a small magazine in the 1970s, when I was in my 20s, called Success Unlimited and being inspired each month to work hard and stay positive. The publisher of this magazine was W. Clement Stone, who started his career selling insurance policies door to door and who went on to build Combined Insurance, which became part of Aon, one of the largest insurance companies in the world.

By the time Mr. Stone died in 2002, he was a very successful businessman, an extremely generous philanthropist and totally committed to spreading the gospel of positive thinking. I remember reading one of his books, The Success System That Never Fails, which was both an autobiography and a blueprint for achieving success. Stone told the story of spending a summer on a farm in Michigan when he was 12, getting fresh air, helping on the farm and enjoying picnics, carnivals and camping out.

W. Clement Stone

"But I'll never forget the first day I went upstairs to the attic," he wrote, "for there I met Horatio Alger. At least 50 of his books, dusty and weather-worn, were piled in the corner. I took one down to the hammock in the front yard and started to read."

Stone said he was so enthralled he couldn't stop. "I read through all of them that summer," he wrote.

He said the principle in each book was that "the hero became a success because he was a man of character -- the villain a failure because he deceived and embezzled. How many Alger books were sold? No one knows. Estimates range from 100 million to 300 million. We do know that his books inspired thousands of American boys from poor families to strive to do the right thing because it was right and to acquire wealth."

That was the first time I had heard of Horatio Alger, but it never occurred to me to try to find his books. Over the years, I founded Creators Syndicate, which became one of the most successful newspaper syndication companies in the world. I attribute much of our success to our positive thinking and upbeat attitude. We became a multimillion-dollar international corporation by syndicating a wide variety of journalists, celebrities and award-winning cartoonists.

As we were expanding into new businesses, e-books and audiobooks were a natural starting point because we work with so many talented writers and artists. But we also wanted to try new things. With that in mind, I remembered Mr. Stone's enthusiastic recommendation of Horatio Alger's books, and I decided to read some. Many were available as e-books, and I thoroughly enjoyed them.

I had a good feeling whenever I was transported back to New York City as it was in 1870, when trains were called "cars" and there were no automobiles. There was a constant risk of crossing the streets without streetlights or walk signs. A number of years later, the Brooklyn Dodgers, now the Los Angeles Dodgers, got their name from the treacherous dodging of horses, wagons and streetcars that was required to cross the street in the city. In those days, plumbing with hot and cold running water was not taken for granted, much less radios, televisions, computers or smartphones. Are you kidding? A smartphone in the 1860s? There wasn't even a telephone.

But what great stories Alger wrote -- one after another. I couldn't get enough of them! And it was impossible not to feel grateful for all the modern conveniences of the 21st century when immersing myself in the world of America as it was in the 1860s and '70s.

As I read book after book, I felt like a teenager all over again, excited about the future and the promise of a brighter tomorrow. It was then that I decided to go full bore into spreading the word of Horatio Alger.

One of the problems with the e-books was the lack of organization; another was the maddening number of typos, over and over and over, or the lack of illustrations or the lack of a table of contents. In fact, what was intended to be a good deed to spread Mr. Alger's message really turned out to be something of a disservice.

So I made it my mission to have professional editors edit the texts so there were no typographical or spelling errors. We found appropriate illustrations. We included detailed tables of contents for each book, and we decided to publish them in groups, when appropriate, which has never been done before. We are including commentaries and teachers guides with each e-book.

We also decided to make audiobooks of as many of these "Stories of Success" as possible. We hired a terrific actor, Ben Gillman, and his initial experience shows you how far we have to go to spread the word. Ben went to the Hollywood public library to find some Horatio Alger books, but there was none. "You'd have to go to the downtown public library, in the historical section, to find those," the librarian told him.

Remember, this is one of the best-selling American authors of all time, yet it is as if he never existed.

Part of the problem is that some of the caricatures of Horatio Alger over the years have been absolutely brutal. Even to this day, the Encyclopedia Britannica, from which we expect objective reporting, calls Alger's dialogue and plots "outrageously bad." Come again? The encyclopedia is supposed to provide broad knowledge on specific subjects, not offer the biased literary criticism of a handful of editors. Talk about being unfair -- and just plain wrong!

How do you answer a cheap shot like that? Really, it is nothing more than an incredibly snooty opinion; in fact, it is an "outrageously bad" opinion. Remember, the Horatio Alger books were intended to be not great literature but rather inspirational stories to motivate young boys to achieve a better life. If the dialogue and plots were not lively and believable, the books would not have sold in the millions. The fact that Horatio Alger helped form the American character shows that an incredible number of boys ate up his books as thrilling and believable.

The brilliant writer Stefan Kanfer wrote an extensive review of Horatio Alger's works in 2000 for City Journal magazine, a publication of the prestigious Manhattan Institute. He started off believing the critics, but when he actually read some of Horatio Alger's books, he drew a totally different conclusion. "I began reading the novels aloud to my children," he wrote. "We found them well-plotted, entertaining, and instructive, not at all the righteous antiquities that I had been led to believe. Almost every chapter ends with a cliff-hanger, and all of us could hardly wait for the next night to find out what happened. The conclusions never failed to produce an emotional satisfaction and a feeling that what the author was selling -- independence, forbearance, square dealing -- was well worth buying."

We can only speculate about why the critics have been so harsh on Horatio Alger, but no doubt some it stems from their being turned off by precisely the character traits that Mr. Kanfer identifies. Like it or not, there is a mindset that scoffs at individual achievement through hard work, a positive attitude and generosity -- living every day with an "attitude of gratitude," which is the essence of Horatio Alger's message.

W. Clement Stone was routinely mocked for starting the day by saying, "I feel healthy! I feel happy! I feel terrific!" He encouraged his employees to do the same. In fact, he encouraged everyone to demonstrate outward enthusiasm and PMA, which stood for a positive mental attitude. His critics thought he was ridiculous, but Mr. Stone got the last laugh, living to age 100, which he had set as his goal, and accumulating hundreds of millions of dollars.

Roswell Crawford is an important character in Ragged Dick and Fame and Fortune because he oozes the world-owes-me-a-living attitude that is so common today. "Roswell was troubled with a large share of pride," Alger writes, "though it might have troubled himself to explain what he had to be proud of."

Roswell never understands the importance of integrity and its relationship to earning one's living. In fact, he once says that he would be happy to be paid $10 a week for nothing. "Well, if I get it, I don't care if I don't earn it," he says. In fact, Roswell is ashamed to be seen in the streets carrying a large bundle as part of a delivery for his job. Before being fired, his boss tells him, "You appear to think yourself of too great consequence to discharge properly the duties of your position."

Contrast that with Richard Hunter's attitude toward his entry-level job when he first starts working at the firm. "I'm ready to do anything that is required of me. I want to make myself useful," he says.

I have the impression that was the same attitude that Horatio Alger had as he approached his goal of becoming a successful writer who could change the world -- or at least the world of the thousands of homeless street urchins in the big city. It is difficult to imagine how bad their plight was. For instance, in 1874, which was seven years after Ragged Dick was first published, there was a little girl named Mary Ellen Wilson, who was beaten unmercifully by her stepmother. She was sent out into the streets ill-clothed in winter. There were other abuses, and they were horrible.

So a social worker named Etta Angel Wheeler wanted to intervene, to help get the child out of that environment. But there were no laws to protect children in such situations. Etta was desperate -- and clever. She enlisted the help of the American Society for the Prevention of Cruelty to Animals because animals were protected by law. Her attorneys argued that Mary Ellen, "as a member of the animal kingdom, deserved the same protection as abused animals." This led to new legislation and various child protective services.

Horatio Alger was at the forefront of this movement. He wanted to help the poor kids in the inner city, and he wound up not only helping them but inspiring millions of other young readers across the country. Many of them transformed their lives as a direct result of the inspiration of the "Stories of Success" that Horatio Alger managed to tell in one exciting setting after another.

It is not surprising that Ernest Hemingway's sister said that her brother could not get enough of Horatio Alger or that Walter Brennan, a famous actor for much of the 20th century, devoured his books. As the legendary Groucho Marx said: "Horatio Alger's books conveyed a powerful message to me and to many of my young friends -- that if you worked hard at your trade, the big chance would eventually come. As a child, I didn't regard it as a myth, and as an old man, I think of it as the story of my life."

Groucho was speaking for millions of Americans in the past and, we hope, millions more in the future.

Rick Newcombe is the founder and CEO of Creators Syndicate, Creators Publishing and Sumner Books.

PREVIEW OF ANOTHER ADVENTURE IN THE HORATIO ALGER "STORIES OF SUCCESS" SERIES

SLOW AND SURE

"It's almost time for Paul to come home," said Mrs. Hoffman. "I must be setting the table for dinner."

"I wonder how he will like my new picture," said Jimmy, a delicate boy of eight, whose refined features, thoughtful look, and high brow showed that his mind by no means shared the weakness of his body. Though only eight years of age he already manifested a remarkable taste and talent for drawing, in which he had acquired surprising skill, considering that he had never taken lessons, but had learned all he knew from copying such pictures as fell in his way.

"Let me see your picture, Jimmy," said Mrs. Hoffman. "Have you finished it?"

She came up and looked over his shoulder. He had been engaged in copying a humorous picture from the last page of Harper's Weekly. It was an ambitious attempt on the part of so young a pupil, but he had succeeded remarkably well, reproducing with close fidelity the grotesque expressions of the figures introduced in the picture.

"That is excellent, Jimmy," said his mother in warm commendation.

The little boy looked gratified.

"Do you think I will be an artist some day?" he asked.

"I have no doubt of it," said his mother, "if you can only obtain suitable instruction. However, there is plenty of time for that. You are only seven years old."

"I shall be eight tomorrow," said Jimmy, straightening up his slender form with the pride which every boy feels in advancing age.

"So you will. I had forgotten it."

"I wonder whether I can earn as much money as Paul when I get as old," said Jimmy thoughtfully. "I don't think I can. I shan't be half as strong."

"It isn't always the strongest who earn the most money," said his mother.

"But Paul is smart as well as strong."

151

"So are you smart. You can read unusually well for a boy of your age, and in drawing I think Paul is hardly your equal, though he is twice as old."

Jimmy laughed.

"That's true, mother," he said. "Paul tried to draw a horse the other day, and it looked more like a cow."

"You see then that we all have our different gifts. Paul has a talent for business."

"I think he'll be rich some day, mother."

"I hope he will, for I think he will make a good use of his money."

While Mrs. Hoffman was speaking she had been setting the table for dinner. The meal was not a luxurious one, but there was no lack of food. Beside rolls and butter, there was a plate of cold meat, an apple pie, and a pot of steaming hot tea. The cloth was scrupulously clean, and I am sure that though the room was a humble one not one of my readers need have felt a repugnance to sitting down at Mrs. Hoffman's plain table.

For the benefit of such as may not have read "Paul the Peddler," I will explain briefly that Mrs. Hoffman, by the death of her husband two years previous, had been reduced to poverty, which compelled her to move into a tenement house and live as best she could on the earnings of her oldest son, Paul, supplemented by the pittance she obtained for sewing. Paul, a smart, enterprising boy, after trying most of the street occupations, had become a young street merchant. By a lucky chance he had obtained capital enough to buy out a necktie stand below the Astor House, where his tact and energy had enabled him to achieve a success, the details of which we will presently give. Besides his own profits, he was able to employ his mother in making neckties at a compensation considerably greater than she could have obtained from the Broadway shops for which she had hitherto worked.

Scarcely was dinner placed on the table when Paul entered. He was a stout, manly boy of fifteen, who would readily have been taken for a year or two older, with a frank, handsome face, and an air of confidence and self-reliance, which he had acquired through his independent efforts to gain a livelihood. He had been thrown upon his own resources at an age when most boys have everything done for them, and though this had been a disadvantage so far as his education was concerned, it had developed in him a confidence in himself and his own ability to cope with the world not usually found in boys of his age.

"Well, mother," said he briskly, "I am glad dinner is ready, for I am as hungry as a wolf."

"I think there will be enough for you," said his mother, smiling. "If not, we will send to the baker's for an extra supply."

"Is a wolf hungry, Paul?" asked Jimmy, soberly accepting Paul's simile.

"I'll draw you one after supper, Jimmy, and you can judge," answered Paul.

"Your animals all look like cows, Paul," said his little brother.

"I see you are jealous of me," said Paul, with much indignation, "because I draw better than you."

"After supper you can look at my last picture," said Jimmy. "It is copied from Harper's Weekly."

"Pass it along now, Jimmy. I don't think it will spoil my appetite."

Jimmy handed it to his brother with a look of pardonable pride.

"Excellent, Jimmy. I couldn't do it better myself," said Paul. "You are a little genius."

"I like drawing so much, Paul. I hope some time I can do something else besides copy."

"No doubt you will. I am sure you will be a famous artist some day, and make no end of money by your pictures."

"That's what I would like—to make money."

"Fie, Jimmy! I had no idea you were so fond of money."

"I would like to help mother just as you are doing, Paul. Do you think I will ever earn as much as you do?"

"A great deal more, I hope, Jimmy. Nevertheless, I am doing well," added Paul in a tone of satisfaction. "Did you know, mother, it is six months today since I bought out the necktie stand?"

"Is it, Paul?" asked his mother with interest. "Have you succeeded as well as you anticipated?"

"Better, mother. It was a good idea putting in a case of knives. They help along my profits. Why, I sold four knives today, making on an average twenty-five cents each."

"Did you? That is indeed worthwhile."

"It is more than I used to average for a whole day's earnings before I went into this business."

"How many neckties did you sell, Paul?" asked Jimmy.

"I sold fourteen."

"How much profit did you make on each?"

"About fourteen cents. Can you tell how much that makes?"

"I could cipher it out on my slate."

"No matter; I'll tell you. It makes a dollar and ninety-six cents. That, added to the money I made on the knives, amounts to two dollars and ninety-six cents."

"Almost three dollars."

"Yes; sometimes I sell more neckties, but then I don't always sell as many knives. However, I am satisfied."

"I have made two dozen neckties today, Paul," said his mother.

"I am afraid you did too much, mother."

"Oh, no. There isn't much work about a necktie."

"Then I owe you a dollar and twenty cents, mother."

"I don't think you ought to pay me five cents apiece, Paul."

"That's fair enough, mother. If I get fourteen cents for selling a tie, certainly you ought to get five cents for making one."

"But your money goes to support us, Paul."

"And where does yours go, mother?"

"A part of it has gone for a new dress, Paul. I went up to Stewart's today and bought a dress pattern. I will show it to you after dinner."

"That's right, mother. You don't buy enough new dresses. Considering that you are the mother of a successful merchant, you ought to dash out. Doesn't Jimmy want some clothes?"

"I am going to buy him a new suit tomorrow. He is eight years old tomorrow."

"Is he? What an old fellow you are getting to be, Jimmy! How many gray hairs have you got?"

"I haven't counted," said Jimmy, laughing.

"I tell you what, mother, we must celebrate Jimmy's birthday. He is the only artist in the family, and we must treat him with proper consideration. I'll tell you what, Jimmy, I'll close up my business at twelve o'clock, and give all my clerks a half-holiday. Then I'll take you and mother to Barnum's Museum, where you can see all the curiosities, and the play besides. How would you like that?"

"Ever so much, Paul," said the little boy, his eyes brightening at the prospect. "There's a giant there, isn't there? How tall is he?"

"Somewhere about eighteen feet, I believe."

"Now you are making fun, Paul."

"Well, it's either eighteen or eight, one or the other. Then there's a dwarf, two feet high, or is it inches?"

"Of course it's feet. He couldn't be so little as two inches."

"Well, Jimmy, I dare say you're right. Then it's settled that we go to the museum tomorrow. You must go with us, mother."

"Oh, yes, I will go," said Mrs. Hoffman, "and I presume I shall enjoy it nearly as much as Jimmy."

BE SURE TO LISTEN TO THE AUDIOBOOK "STORIES OF SUCCESS" SERIES BY HORATIO ALGER, AVAILABLE ON AUDIBLE.COM AND ITUNES. GO TO WWW.SUMNERBOOKS.COM.

www.ingramcontent.com/pod-product-compliance
Lightning Source LLC
Chambersburg PA
CBHW071254130626

46556CB00003B/1312